Published by Ideals Children's Books
An imprint of Hambleton-Hill Publishing, Inc.
Nashville, Tennessee 37218

Printed and bound in the United States of America

ISBN 1-57102-301-1

Graphic Design/Art Direction
John Laughlin

Photography
Scott Bonner

Blackstone Magik Enterprises, Inc.
Licensor

Williams-Bell & Associates, Inc.
Packager

EVERYDAY MAGIC

The BLACKSTONE Family Magic Shoppe

By Bellamie Blackstone

Ideals Children's Books • Nashville, Tennessee
an imprint of Hambleton-Hill Publishing, Inc.

As a young man growing up in the world of magic, my father was America's leading illusionist from 1918 until 1963. Although I enjoyed watching the big shows, some of my fondest memories were of sitting around the dining room table with my father and his friends as they did their versions of "betchas." Many of these tricks used coins. As we traveled all over the world, the coins we used were often foreign and very exotic, but simple U.S. pennies, nickels, and dimes work equally well. Betchas were practiced in trains, cars, planes, hotels, and at dinner tables around the world.

—Harry Blackstone, Jr.

EVERYDAY MAGIC

Paper clips soar through the air like Robin Hood's arrows!

YOU NEED:
- a dollar bill
- 2 paper clips
- an audience

1. Announce that you can make a paper clip fly like an arrow.

2. Remove a dollar bill from your pocket and fold it in half.

3. Slip a paper clip over the center of the fold, and then jerk the bill open (*Figures 1 & 2*). The paper clip will fly off just like an arrow from a bow.

4. Now tell your audience that you can even do Robin Hood's trick—the one where he split one arrow with a second. Say, *"I betcha I can shoot two paper clips off this dollar bill and wind up with them at least touching each other."*

5. Fold the dollar bill into three vertical sections—like an accordion (*Figure 3*). Fasten it with two paper clips (*Figure 4*).

6. Quickly pull the two top corners of the bill. The paper clips will not only fly off the bill, but they'll become linked in the process!

Props are anything used during a performance.

Figure 1

Figure 2

Figure 3

Figure 4

*Don't be afraid to add your own personality
to your performances.*

A piece of paper and this play on words will keep your friends guessing.

YOU NEED:
- a piece of paper
- a quarter
- a pencil
- a friend

Say to a friend, *"I betcha I can cut a hole in a piece of paper the same size as a dime and push a quarter through it without tearing the paper."*

He may say that he already knows how to do this. If so, ask him to show you. He will probably do one of two things. No matter which one he does, tell him that that is the old way, and you have an entirely different technique. Then show him one of these two techniques.

Technique A

1. Tear a hole in the paper about the size of a dime (*Figure 1*).

2. Put the quarter on the table.

3. Stick a pencil through the hole in the paper. Then push the quarter around with it (*Figure 2*).

Perception *is how the brain interprets the information it receives from the five senses.*

Figure 1

Figure 2

Technique B

1. Tear a hole in the paper about the size of a dime (*Figure 1*).

2. Fold the paper in half through the center of the hole and drop the quarter inside (*Figure 3*).

3. Hold each end of the crease and lever upward (*Figure 4*), using the hole as the center of the bend. The hole will stretch open and the quarter will drop through (*Figure 5*)!

Figure 3

Figure 4

Figure 5

As part of your performance, get your audience to guess how a trick works—just be sure not to reveal the secret.

Move a dime across the table without ever touching it.

YOU NEED:
- a table covered with a tablecloth
- a dime and 2 nickels
- an empty glass
- an audience

1. Say to your audience, *"After long study and practice, I have learned how to move objects without ever touching them. I'll prove it."*

2. Place a dime on the tablecloth with a nickel on each side of it (*Figure 1*).

3. Place the glass upside down so that it rests on the two nickels (*Figure 2*).

4. Now say, *"I will remove that dime from under the glass without ever touching the nickels or the glass."*

The Secret

5. Start scratching the tablecloth just outside the glass (*Figure 3*). The dime will "walk" right into your waiting fingers!

Magicians' tricks rely heavily upon tricking the eye.

Figure 1

Figure 2

Figure 3

Optical illusions *are images that misguide the brain.*

Move a coin without ever touching it!

YOU NEED:
- a table
- a dime, nickel, and penny
- an audience

1. Place a dime and a nickel on a table so that their edges are touching (*Figure 1*).

2. Say to your audience, *"I betcha I can put a penny in between these two coins, without moving the dime or touching the nickel in any way."*

3. Put the penny on the table next to the dime (*Figure 2*).

4. Put one index finger on top of the dime, and, without moving it, press it hard against the tabletop (*Figure 3*).

5. Put your other index finger on top of the penny, and slide it fast and hard against the dime (*Figure 4*). The force will knock the nickel away from the dime.

6. Now simply slide the penny in between the nickel and dime.

Note: This trick works best on a smooth surface.

The easiest way to make a small movement without being detected is to cover it with a larger movement.

Figure 1

Figure 2

Figure 3

Figure 4

A sleight of hand *is a secret move that your audience does not see.*

Give your friends a quick lesson in counting.

YOU NEED:
- 10 coins
- 3 empty glasses
- a friend

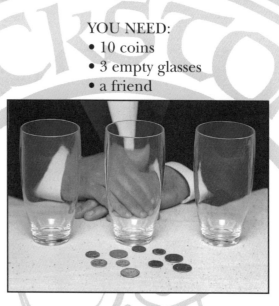

Say to a friend, *"I betcha you can't divide these ten coins into these three glasses so that there's an odd number of coins in each glass."*

After a number of tries she will finally tell you that it can't be done. She'll probably insist that no one can do it. Then show her how it's done.

1. Put three coins in the first glass (*Figure 1*).

2. Put two coins in the second glass (*Figure 2*).

3. Put five coins in the third glass (*Figure 3*).

At this point your friend may say, *"Can't you count? You put two coins in one glass. That's not an odd number."*

The Secret

4. Slowly pick up the third glass and put it inside the second glass (*Figure 4*). Each glass now contains an odd number of coins.

The fluidness of a magician's moves is more important than his haste.

Figure 1

Figure 2

Figure 3

Figure 4

*A clever device that is not seen by the audience
is called a gimmick.*

Your friends will be easily caught with this play on words.

YOU NEED:
- a penny
- a dime
- a friend

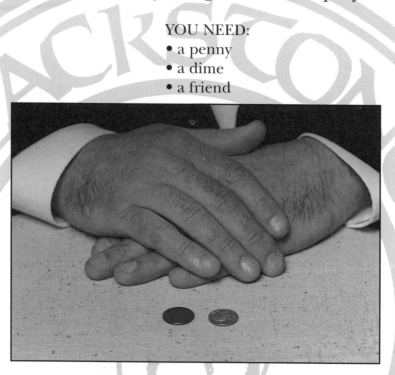

1. Say to a friend, *"I have two coins inside my fist. The two coins total eleven cents, but one of them is not a dime! I betcha you can't guess what I'm holding (Figure 1)."*

2. After all the usual guesses about British two-penny coins and other wrong answers, you're ready to make your move. Slap the two coins—a penny and a dime—down on the table *(Figure 2)*.

3. In answer to your friend's statement, which will surely start with, *"But you said . . . ,"* your reply is, *"No, I'm right. One of them isn't a dime, it's a penny!"*

In medieval times, spectators believed that supernatural forces helped magicians perform their magic.

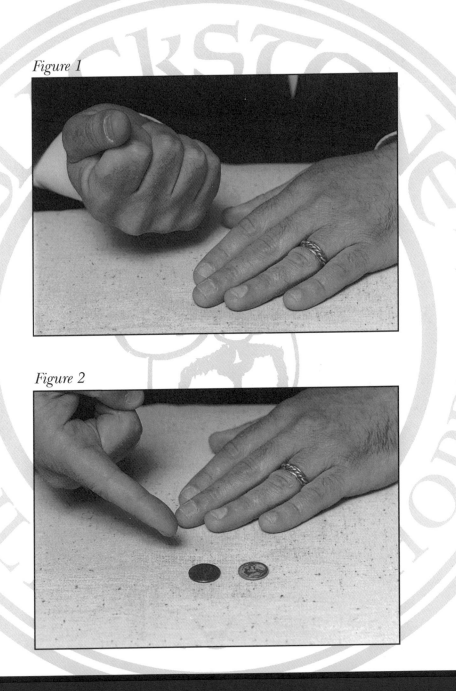

Figure 1

Figure 2

A magic wand *should be used to divert*
an audience's attention.

You can't lose with this guessing game.

YOU NEED:
- several dimes
- several quarters
- an audience

1. Say to your audience, *"A few months ago I read in the newspaper that a rare penny had sold for $500. Since then I've been studying coins and I've really learned quite a lot. For example, if someone put a quarter facedown in front of me, I could name the date it was minted. In fact, I'm so sure of my skill that I will give you a dime for every quarter that I guess wrong."*

(Have several dimes ready because there's going to be some fast shuffling in a few moments.)

2. After all the quarters have been put facedown in front of you, stare intently at the first one.

3. Name a date and turn the coin over. If you've guessed right, great! If you've guessed wrong, put a dime down on the table and pull the quarter toward you. Continue this with the rest of the quarters until you've finished.

4. Then go back and pick up each quarter that was a wrong guess and put them in your pocket. Didn't you say you'd give them a dime for every quarter you guessed wrong? (Be sure to return the quarters once the trick is over!)

Never reveal the secrets behind your tricks.

A little misdirection can go a long way.

YOU NEED:
- a handkerchief
- 50 cents
- a friend with 50 cents

This one has to be done very slowly so that your friend can see that you aren't pulling any sleight-of-hand tricks on her.

1. Drop 50 cents on to an empty handkerchief.

2. Have your friend drop her 50 cents on to the handkerchief also.

3. Gather up the four corners like a bag and shake it a couple of times so that she can hear the money rattle inside.

4. Say to her, *"Do you hear the coins? They're clinking, so they must all be in there, right? All right, would you pay 75 cents for the dollar inside this handkerchief?"*

5. Continue shaking the bag as you say this. When she says yes, smile and say, *"You mean you would pay 25 cents to get your own 50 cents back?"*

Practice your tricks until you are perfectly comfortable performing them.

It's raining quarters!

YOU NEED:
- 3 quarters
- a friend

1. Have your friend hold his arm out in front of himself with his hand out flat, fingers together and flat, and palm facing the floor.

2. Put a quarter on his knuckles and a second one near his wrist (*Figure 1*).

3. Ask your friend to flip the two coins into the air and catch them one at a time before they hit the floor. He will do so, and then wonder what was so hard about that.

4. Not a thing, you reply, as you now put three coins on the back of his hand, one each on the wrist, knuckles, and fingertips (*Figure 2*). On the first toss your friend will be in deep water. He may hit the third coin, but he will have a hard time actually catching it.

5. Now put the three coins on your own arm. Toss them up and, to your friend's amazement, catch them with ease.

Never perform the same trick twice in one show.

The Secret

To catch all three coins at once, bend your knees and dip your body as the coins fall. When you do this you will have practically no trouble catching them. Be sure to practice ahead of time, so that it becomes a natural action for you.

If you want to make absolutely sure no one can match you, practice with four coins!

Figure 1   *Figure 2*

Adding a simple wave of a magic wand can greatly add to the professional look of your performance.

Test a friend's physical condition and reflexes.

YOU NEED:
- a dollar bill
- a friend

1. Put a lengthwise crease in a new dollar bill.

2. Hold it by one end in a vertical position in your right hand (*Figure 1*).

3. Hold the thumb and index finger of your left hand about an inch apart.

4. Place them halfway between the portrait and the bottom end of the bill (*Figure 1*).

5. Drop the bill and catch it with your left hand (*Figure 2*).

6. Do it again so that your friend can see how easily you do it, and then ask her to do the same. She will most likely place her finger and thumb on either side of the bill where you had yours. Tell her that you're going to drop the bill and see if she can catch it. It can't be done!

For early magicians there was no guidebook.
Secrets were simply passed from
generation to generation.

Figure 1

Figure 2

During colonial times in North America all types of
entertainment were prohibited—including magician's
performances—as there was much work to be done.

Prove that you can't be pushed around.

YOU NEED:
- a dollar bill
- a door
- a friend

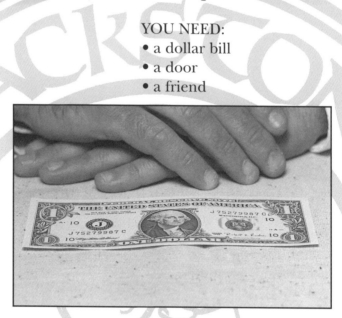

1. Take out a dollar bill and say to a friend, *"I betcha that if I stand on one end of this dollar bill and you stand on the other, you can't knock me off my end."*

2. When she accepts your challenge, place the bill on the floor in the center of a doorway. (Make sure the door closes from your side.)

3. Have your friend stand on the last two inches of her end of the bill.

4. Close the door and stand on your end. Now it's impossible for her to knock you off!

The March 18, 1734, edition of the Weekly Journal *was the first American newspaper to feature an ad for a magician.*

Your friends will need to polish their listening skills for this one!

YOU NEED:
- 4 quarters
- a plate
- a friend

1. For this trick, tell a friend that you have a simple counting problem that no one seems to be able to solve.

2. While you're talking, slowly count four quarters on to the table, one at a time (*Figure 1*).

3. Challenge your friend to pick the four quarters up off the table, count them one at a time on to a plate, then pick them all up again, one at a time, and still have one left on the plate. (This one usually works best if you try to hurry your friend. Working under pressure keeps him from realizing the simplicity of the setup.)

The Secret

4. When he gives up and it's your turn, openly count the four quarters on to the plate.

5. Now remove three of the coins, one at a time (*Figure 2*).

6. Then pick up the plate with the last quarter still on it (*Figure 3*).

Figure 1   Figure 2   Figure 3

In the 1800s, many magicians gave away prizes to lure people to their shows. Gifts included everything from furniture and flour to live pigs!

Toe-touching becomes an impossible task!

YOU NEED:
- a dollar bill
- a friend

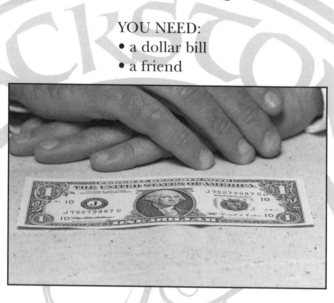

1. Ask a friend if he can touch his toes without bending his knees. When he says yes, ask him to show you. No matter how perfectly he does it, tell him that you saw his knees bend. You, however, have a fair test that will make absolutely sure that his knees stay ruler straight.

2. Put your friend against a wall so that his heels and back are touching the wall.

3. Then lay out a dollar bill on the floor just in front of his toes.

4. Tell him to reach down, without bending his knees, and pick up the dollar. It's impossible!

Pulling a rabbit out of a hat, one of the most celebrated of all tricks, first appeared in the late 1830s.

Can you predict which way the coin will land?

YOU NEED:
- a coin
- a friend

1. Everyone knows that when you flip a coin once, there is an equal chance that it will come up heads or tails.

2. But how many people could resist the challenge if you were to say, *"I betcha when I toss this coin I can correctly guess which way it will land two out of three times."* After all, everyone knows that it's harder to be right two out of three times.

3. Well, anyone who can't resist this challenge will end up a loser. The fact is that this is still an even chance, because one or the other of you will have to be right at least two out of three times. If you're not right, then the other person has to be right two out of three times.

Magicians were often called upon by royalty to perform their conjuring acts.

"Magically" tell the date by only looking at the tails side of a coin.

YOU NEED:
- a quarter
- a friend

1. Ask a friend if she has a quarter you can borrow for a demonstration.

2. Take the quarter in your hand and, without looking at it, start rubbing it between your fingers.

3. After a moment, nod your head in satisfaction and return the quarter to your friend.

4. Then say, *"I betcha that if you put a quarter facedown in the palm of my hand, I can tell you the date just by looking at the tails side."*

5. When your friend puts the quarter back in your hand, gaze intently at the coin, as if you are trying to see through it.

6. Then . . . loudly call out today's date!

Many master magicians of the eighteenth and nineteenth centuries were impersonated by aspiring magicians.

*Force your friend to turn over the first face card–
without him even realizing it.*

YOU NEED:
- a deck of cards
- a friend

1. Say to a friend, *"I betcha that you will turn up a face card (a King, Queen, or Jack) before I do."*

2. Ask him to shuffle a deck of cards and cut it into piles (*Figure 1*). Each of you then takes a pile and you both begin to turn over the cards one at a time.

The Secret

3. When you get your packet of cards hold them facedown in your left hand. As your right hand removes each card, tip it slightly so that you can see its face, then turn it faceup on the table (*Figure 2*). Don't be sneaky about it, just pretend you are checking to see if you're going to get "struck."

4. As soon as you see a face card, deal it facedown on the table. Nine times out of ten your opponent will give a cry of triumph and turn the card over to show you that it's a face card. You win the betcha because *he* turned the card faceup, not you!

Figure 1   *Figure 2*

Women were often used in magicians' acts—whether they were vanishing, being sawed in half, or relaying what they saw through their second sight.

Baffle your friends with this simple subtraction problem.

YOU NEED:
- a piece of paper
  (either a square or rectangle)
- a pencil or pen
- a friend

1. Show your friend a piece of paper and a pen (or pencil).

2. Then say, *"I betcha I can take four away from four and leave eight. And I betcha that you can't do it."*

3. She will try, of course. And after she has used Roman numerals, Arabic figures, and algebra she'll give up.

4. Pick up the paper and tear off each of the four corners (*Figure 1*). Presto! You've taken four from four and gotten eight—corners, that is!

Figure 1

Mission accomplished!

"Hypnotizing a Duck" and "The Indian Rope Trick" were two of master magician Howard Thurston's specialties.

Tricking your friends is as easy as learning your A, B, Cs!

YOU NEED:
• a friend

1. Challenge a friend to a duel of speech.

2. Tell her that you can say the alphabet backward faster than she can.

3. When she has accepted the contest, face your friend and ask for someone to give the starting signal.

4. As soon as the start signal is given, turn your back on her and say the alphabet in the normal manner (A, B, C, D, etc.). You *did* promise to say it backward, didn't you?

The Magic Circle of London is a well-respected society for amateur and professional magicians.

Roll your hands around a pencil without dropping it.

YOU NEED:
- a pencil
- a friend

1. Place your palms together with your fingers outstretched and with a pencil crosswise in the crotch of your thumbs (*Figure 1*).

2. Ask your friend to watch closely as you roll your hands around each other so that when you finish, both thumbs are back on top and your palms are together again. Ask your friend to try to roll his hands around the pencil. He will fail and usually wind up just short of a dislocated wrist.

The Secret

3. Start with the point of the pencil pointing to the right.

4. Slide your right thumb to the left so it goes in between the knuckle of the index finger and the thumb of your left hand, but keep your palms together (*Figure 2*).

5. Slide the fingers of your left hand up toward the ceiling as you rotate each thumb around the other (*Figure 3*).

6. Let the point of the pencil slide under your left fingers as your palms rotate around the pencil (*Figure 4*). You should wind up with both thumbs below the pencil and both palms facing the floor.

7. To continue, use the same thumb-around-thumb action. Rotate your palms around the pencil, letting the eraser end slide up between your two palms and past your left fingers (*Figures 5 & 6*). You should finish back in the original position. Now hand the pencil to someone else so you can watch the fun!

Las Vegas, Nevada is considered by many to be the Capital of Magic.

Figure 1

Figure 2

Figure 3

Figure 4

Figure 5

Figure 6

As part of a magician's show, large animals such as
tigers and elephants are often made
to vanish and reappear.

Challenge your friends with this twirling scissors trick.

YOU NEED:
- a pair of blunt scissors
- a friend

1. Challenge a friend to twirl a pair of scissors like this:

a. Have your friend hold both hands in front of him with his fingers out flat and his palms toward the ceiling.

b. Put each of his little fingers through one of the handles of a pair of blunt scissors so that the ends hang down.

c. Have him swing the blunt points of the scissors upward and around toward himself until they make one and a half revolutions. When he's finished, the blunt points of the scissors should end up pointing toward the ceiling and the backs of his hands should be touching.

He will try and try, but the best he will be able to do is get the scissors halfway around before they fall. You, of course, know the secret, so take the scissors and show him that you can do it with ease.

Some magicians use stunt doubles for their more dangerous feats, but many perform their own stunts.

The Secret

1. When you first swing the scissors toward you, let them slide toward the fingernail of each little finger (*Figure 1*).

2. At the same time, touch each little finger to your palm. The scissors will slide along the finger until each handle is also touching the palm (*Figure 2*).

3. Lock each little finger on to its scissor handle and keep rotating your hands (*Figure 3*). You'll finish with your hands back to back and the blunt points of the scissors straight up (*Figure 4*). (But don't tell your friend how it's done!)

Figure 1

Figure 2

Figure 3

Figure 4

Magic challenges the imagination.

*An ordinary pencil mysteriously clings to the palm
of your hand—one of the oldest published tricks in magic.*

YOU NEED:
- a pencil
- an audience

Note: For this trick refer to figures on pages 40 and 41.

1. Show the pencil and your left hand to the audience so they can see that there are no sticky substances or threads hidden in your fingers (*Figure 1*).

2. Hold your left hand palm up, and place the pencil on it (*Figure 2*).

3. Close your left fingers over the pencil. (Note: For clarity of description, the photos are shown with the palm open.)

4. Grab your left wrist with your right hand "to steady it" (*Figure 3*). (Note: The right thumb is on top and the fingers are underneath.)

5. Stare intently at the pencil. Now you will make the important "move" that creates the illusion.

Magic defies language and cultural barriers.

6. Turn your left hand so that it is palm down. Let your left wrist turn within your right fingers so that when your left hand is palm down, the right hand is still holding your left wrist with the thumb on top and fingers underneath. As you turn your left hand, withdraw your right forefinger from the wrist. The audience does not see this move because they are concentrating on the pencil. On the other side of your closed hand, your right forefinger should be holding the pencil against your left palm, even though your left fingers are loosely closed (*Figures 4 through 6*).

7. Now, call attention to the amazing event that is about to take place. Slowly and dramatically open your left fingers, holding your left hand palm downward and parallel to the floor. The pencil is mysteriously stuck to your palm. (The audience does not see your right forefinger holding the pencil in place.) The pencil is held in place by the very tip of the finger. From the audience view it seems impossible that the finger could be holding the pencil in place (*Figure 7*).

8. Explain that "magical magnetism" is holding the pencil on the palm but, at the audience's command, the magnetism will stop. Tell someone to say, "Now," anytime she wishes to stop the magnetism. When the word is spoken, let the pencil drop. At this moment, all eyes will be on the pencil. Take advantage of the misdirection and replace your forefinger on the left wrist where it was originally. Slowly turn the left hand palm up (*Figure 7*).

Remember, there are no self-working magic tricks. To present this illusion effectively, as with all illusions, practice is required. Do it over and over again in front of a mirror to get the action and the timing right.

Some ancient cave paintings are believed to show scenes that involve magic.

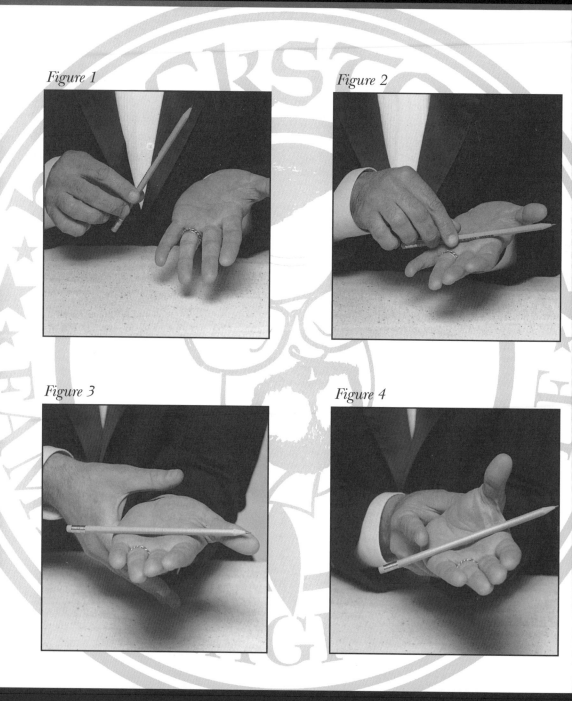

Figure 1

Figure 2

Figure 3

Figure 4

Magicians were often accused of witchcraft and sorcery.

Figure 5

Figure 6

Figure 7

Audiences usually only remember the overall trick, not the essential details.

Magically push a pencil through the center of a handkerchief—without leaving a hole in the cloth.

YOU NEED:
- a pencil (the longer, the better)
- a handkerchief
- an audience

Note: For this trick refer to figures on pages 44 and 45.

1. Hold the pencil in your right hand and have someone from your audience drape the handkerchief over it. Arrange the handkerchief so that the center of one of its sides is directly facing you (*Figure 1*). Show the draped pencil from all sides.

2. As you are showing the pencil, arrange your right-hand grip on it so that the pencil is held between the second and third fingers of your right hand with your thumb to steady it (*Figure 2*).

3. Have several people from your audience feel the top of the pencil through the handkerchief.

The Art of Jugling [sic], published in 1612, is the first book written in English that is dedicated to magic.

4. Now, look at the audience (do *not* look at the draped handkerchief). Tell them that they are about to see something that is impossible. As you talk to them look them in the eye, so that they will look at you and not the handkerchief. Grip the top of the cloth (where it is draped over the top of the pencil) with your left hand. Use the second and third fingers of your right hand to tilt the pencil straight back toward you (*Figure 3*). (This cannot be seen by the spectators because it is behind the handkerchief.)

5. Put your right thumb under the pencil and push it right back up again, only now it is *outside* of the handkerchief (*Figure 4*). This simple move takes only an instant and is done while you are misdirecting the audience's attention by talking and making eye contact with them.

6. When the pencil is put in an up-and-down position, it is immediately held in place behind the handkerchief with your right thumb. (Make sure the top of the handkerchief still drapes over the pencil.) Move your left hand away as if to make a gesture. To the audience, it looks just as if you are holding the draped pencil.

7. Close your left hand into a fist around the pencil and cloth. Reach under the cloth with your right hand and push the pencil up. As it comes up, it will look as if it is penetrating right through the center of the handkerchief (*Figures 5, 6, and 7*).

8. When the pencil is completely pushed up, take it with your right hand and give it to the audience for examination. Show the handkerchief on both sides and give it out also. They will look for a hole in it and will be completely amazed when they can't find one (*Figure 8*).

Ventriloquism *is considered to be magic as many people believe that a ventriloquist can indeed throw his voice.*

Figure 1

Figure 2

Figure 3

Figure 4

Prestidigitation *means sleight of hand.*
It was Jules de Rovère, an aristocrat,
who first coined the term.

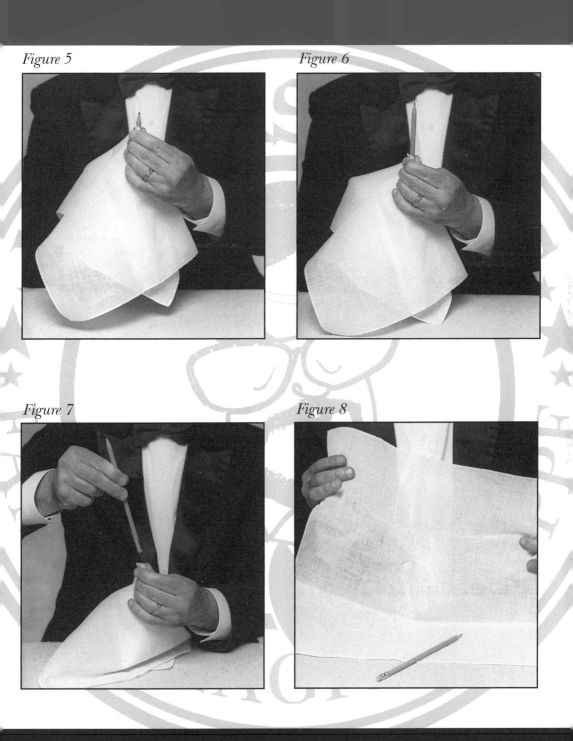

Figure 5

Figure 6

Figure 7

Figure 8

Legerdemain *is another term for the sleights of hand and other tricks of a stage magician.*

Now here's a way to trick three of your friends at once and prove how strong you are!

YOU NEED:
- a broom
- a 6-inch circle of paper
- 3 friends

1. Say to your friends, *"I betcha I'm the world's strongest person, and I can prove it with this broom. With three of you holding one end and me all alone on the other, I betcha I can keep you from pushing my end into a six-inch circle on the floor. That's right, the three of you against poor, weak, little old me."*

2. Lay the target circle on the floor.

3. Have your friends hold the broom with the straws pointing toward the ceiling. Their hands should be just below the straws of the broom.

4. Start with the end of the broom handle about 18 inches above the target.

5. Place the palm of your open hand against the end of the broom handle.

6. Now tell your friends to try to push your end of the broom into the target.

7. To stop them, all you have to do is simply push the end of the handle sideways, easily keeping it outside the circle!

Vaudeville *is a stage show featuring a variety of different acts, including singing, dancing, comedy skits, acrobatics, and more.*

*Here's a trick that will leave your friends
huffing and puffing, while you stay calm and cool.*

YOU NEED:
- a broom
- a friend

1. Find a broom and have a friend hold it horizontally with her hands slightly farther apart than her shoulders. (You can force her to hold the broom in this way by holding your hands so that your fists are opposite her shoulders and her hands are on the outside of yours.)

2. Close each of your hands into a fist with the thumb pointing straight up and then put them against the broom, about six inches on each side of the center.

3. When you're ready, say to your friend, *"I betcha you can't knock me off balance by pushing against my hands with the broom."*

4. You are easily able to resist her strongest efforts because when she begins pushing against your thumbs, you simply push upward with your fists. Each of her arms is being directed slightly outward, and her remaining strength is being pushed so that all her force is split in three directions at once and easily resisted.

Shadowgraphs *are shadows that are cast on a screen as the performer uses his hands to form various silhouettes of animals, birds, and humans.*

This book is dedicated
to the memory of
Harry Blackstone, Jr.
1934 – 1997

Samsung Galaxy® S10

by Bill Hughes

for
dummies®
A Wiley Brand

Samsung Galaxy® S10 For Dummies®

Published by: **John Wiley & Sons, Inc.,** 111 River Street, Hoboken, NJ 07030-5774, www.wiley.com

For general information on our other products and services, please contact our Customer Care Department within the U.S. at 877-762-2974, outside the U.S. at 317-572-3993, or fax 317-572-4002. For technical support, please visit https://hub.wiley.com/community/support/dummies.

Wiley publishes in a variety of print and electronic formats and by print-on-demand. Some material included with standard print versions of this book may not be included in e-books or in print-on-demand. If this book refers to media such as a CD or DVD that is not included in the version you purchased, you may download this material at http://booksupport.wiley.com. For more information about Wiley products, visit www.wiley.com.

Library of Congress Control Number: 2019940130

ISBN 978-1-119-57939-7 (pbk); ISBN 978-1-119-57943-4 (ebk); ISBN 978-1-119-57944-1 (ebk)

Manufactured in the United States of America

C10009973_050119

Contents at a Glance

Table of Contents

Introduction

The Samsung Galaxy S10, S10E, and S10+ are powerful smartphones, among the most powerful mobile phones ever sold. As of the publication of this book, the Galaxy S10s are the standard against which all other Android-based phones are measured.

Each cellular carrier offers a slightly customized version of the Galaxy S10 line-up. Some phones from cellular carriers come out of the box with preloaded applications, games, or files. Most come with accessories, such as a corded headset; others don't. This book doesn't dwell on these kinds of differences.

The name for each network is different, these phones are largely the same. (At least one marketing person at each cellular carrier is cringing as you read this.) This similarity allows me to write this book in a way that covers the common capabilities.

At a more core level, these phones are built for high-speed wireless communications. The cellular carriers have spent kajillions upgrading their networks to offer more coverage and better data speeds than their competition. Again, this book doesn't dwell on these differences in network technology because they don't really make much difference. (Again, at least one engineering person at each cellular carrier is cringing as you read this.)

Similarly, most of the capabilities among the different Galaxy S10 models are similar. The S10+ has a bigger screen, a bigger battery, and more camera lenses than the S10. Similarly, the S10 has a bigger screen, a bigger battery, and more camera lenses than the S10E. Otherwise, the three versions of the Galaxy S10 are practically identical. When there is an important distinction between the S10+, the S10, and the S10E, I will mention it. Otherwise, I will just call the phone the Galaxy S10.

I assume that you already have a Galaxy S10, and I just hope that you have good coverage where you spend more of your time with your phone. If so, you'll be fine. If not, you need to switch to another network; otherwise, the experience with your phone will be frustrating. I would advise you to return your phone to that carrier and buy your Galaxy S10 at another cellular carrier. As long as you have good cellular data coverage, owning a Samsung Galaxy S10 will be an exciting experience!

First, in much the same way that different brands of PCs are all based on the Microsoft Windows operating system, all Galaxy S phones use the Google Android platform. The good news is that the Android platform has proven to be widely popular, even more successful than Google originally expected when it first announced Android in November 2007. More people are using Android-based phones, and more third parties are writing applications. This is good news because it offers you more options for applications (more on this in Chapter 8 on the Play Store, where you buy applications).

In addition, all Galaxy S10 phones use a powerful graphics processor, employ Samsung's Super AMOLED touchscreen, and are covered in Corning's Gorilla Glass. The superior screen experience differentiates this product line from other Android phones. Because of these enhanced capabilities, you can navigate around the screen with multi-touch screen gestures instead of the hierarchical menus found on lesser Android phones. Plus, the videos look stunning from many angles.

Smartphones are getting smarter all the time, and the Galaxy S10 is one of the smartest. However, just because you've used a smartphone in the past doesn't mean you should expect to use your new Galaxy S10 without a bit of guidance.

You may not be familiar with using a multi-touch screen, and your new phone offers a lot of capabilities that you may or may not be familiar with. There used to be a physical button on the front to bring you back to the Home screen. It's no longer a physical button; instead, it's now software based. It would be unfortunate to find out from a kid in the neighborhood that the phone you've been carrying around for several months could solve a problem you've been having because you were never told that the solution was in your pocket the whole time.

In fact, Samsung is proud of the usability of its entire Galaxy line-up — and proud that the user's manual is really just a quick start guide. You can find lots of instructions on the web. However, you have to know what you don't know to get what you want unless you plan to view every tutorial.

That's where this book comes in. This book is a hands-on guide to getting the most out of your Galaxy S10.

About This Book

This book is a reference — you don't have to read it from beginning to end to get all you need out of it. The information is clearly organized and easy to access. You don't need thick glasses to understand this book. This book helps you figure out what you want to do — and then tells you how to do it in plain English.

Within this book, you may note that some web addresses break across two lines of text. If you're reading this book in print and want to visit one of these web pages, simply key in the web address exactly as it's noted in the text, pretending as though the line break doesn't exist. If you're reading this as an e-book, you've got it easy — just click the web address to be taken directly to the web page.

Foolish Assumptions

You know what they say about assuming, so I don't do much of it in this book. But I do make a few assumptions about you:

>> **You have a Galaxy S10 phone.** You may be thinking about buying a Galaxy S10 phone, but my money's on your already owning one. After all, getting your hands on the phone is the best part!

>> **You're not totally new to mobile phones.** You know that your Galaxy S10 phone is capable of doing more than the average phone, and you're eager to find out what your phone can do.

>> **You've used a computer.** You don't have to be a computer expert, but you at least know how to check your email and surf the web.

Icons Used in This Book

Throughout this book, I used *icons* (little pictures in the margin) to draw your attention to various types of information. Here's a key to what those icons mean:

TIP

This whole book is like one big series of tips. When I share especially useful tips and tricks, I mark them with the Tip icon.

REMEMBER

This book is a reference, which means you don't have to commit it to memory — there is no test at the end. But once in a while, I do tell you things that are so important that I think you should remember them, and when I do, I mark them with the Remember icon.

WARNING

Whenever you may do something that could cause a major headache, I warn you with the, er, Warning icon.

TECHNICAL STUFF

These sections provide a little more information than is necessary to use your phone. The hope is that these sections convey extra knowledge to help you understand what is going on when things go wrong, or at least differently than you might have expected.

Beyond the Book

In addition to what you're reading right now, this product also comes with a free access-anywhere Cheat Sheet. To get to this Cheat Sheet, simply go to www. dummies.com and type **Samsung Galaxy S10 For Dummies Cheat Sheet** in the Search box.

Where to Go from Here

You don't have to read this book from cover to cover. You can skip around as you like. For example, if you need the basics on calling, texting, and emailing, turn to Part 2. To discover more about photos, games, and apps, go to Part 4.

Many readers are already somewhat familiar with smartphones and won't need the basic information found in Parts 1 and 2. A reasonably astute mobile phone user can figure out how to use the phone, text, and data capabilities. Parts 1 and 2 are not for those readers. For them, I recommend skipping ahead to the chapters in Parts 3 through 6.

Former iPhone users, on the other hand, are a special case. (First, welcome to the world of Android!) The reality is that the iPhone and Galaxy S series have very similar capabilities, but these functions are just done in slightly different ways and emphasize different approaches to the similar problems. iPhone users, don't worry if you find that this book spends a fair amount of time explaining capabilities with which you're familiar. You can read through those chapters quickly, focus on the *how* instead of the description of *what*, and bypass potential frustration.

Current Samsung Galaxy S9 users are also a special case. The Samsung Galaxy S10 is very similar to the Galaxy S9 in many ways. Galaxy S10 operates mostly like the S9, but has improvements in usability, power consumption, and performance. Plus, the camera has even more capabilities (if you can believe it!). If you're comfortable with the Galaxy S9 and now have a Galaxy S10, Chapters 15 and beyond will be of interest to you.

The majority of readers of this book are actually very astute and get the fact that this book covers the basics of using the Samsung Galaxy S10. A subset of readers complain in Internet reviews that a *For Dummies* book is too basic. If you do this, people will know that you did not read the title. Be sure to read the title and avoid public embarrassment.

1

Getting Started with the Samsung Galaxy S10

Review the capabilities of cellphones and what sets smartphones apart.

Turn off your phone and manage sleep mode.

Chapter **1**

Exploring What You Can Do with Your Phone

Whether you want just the basics from a mobile phone (make and take phone calls, customize your ringtone, take some pictures, maybe use a Bluetooth headset) or you want your phone to be always by your side (a tool for multiple uses throughout your day), you can make that happen. In this chapter, I outline all the things your Samsung Galaxy S10 can do — from the basics to what makes Galaxy S10 phones different from the rest.

Discovering the Basics of Your Phone

All mobile phones on the market today include basic functions, and even some entry-level phones are a little more sophisticated. Of course, Samsung includes all basic functions on the Galaxy S10 model. In addition to making and taking calls (see Chapter 3) and sending and receiving texts (see Chapter 4), the Galaxy S10 sports the following basic features:

» **16MP digital camera:** This resolution is more than enough for posting good-quality images on the Internet and even having 8-x-10-inch prints made.

There is also a front-facing camera with 10MP that is useful for videoconference calls and selfies. Your phone has some amazing capabilities (see Chapter 9 for more information).

» **Ringtones:** You can replace the standard ringtone with custom ringtones that you download to your phone. You also can specify different rings for different numbers.

» **Bluetooth:** The Galaxy S10 phone supports stereo and standard Bluetooth devices. (See Chapter 3 for more on Bluetooth.)

» **High-resolution screen:** The Galaxy S10 and S10+ offer the highest-resolution touchscreens on the market (3,200 x 1,800 pixels); the S10E is not too far behind, with full HD+ resolution.

» **Capacitive touchscreen:** The Galaxy S10 phone offers a very slick touchscreen that's sensitive enough to allow you to interact with the screen accurately, but not so sensitive that it's hard to manage. In addition, it has an optional setting that steps up the sensitivity for special circumstances, like when you want to use one hand!

Taking Your Phone to the Next Level: The Smartphone Features

In addition to the basic capabilities of any entry-level phone, the Galaxy S10, which is based on the popular Android platform for mobile devices, has capabilities associated with other smartphones, such as the Apple iPhone:

» **Internet access:** Access websites through a web browser on your phone.

» **Photos:** The Galaxy S10 comes with a very intelligent camera that has millions of combinations of settings, filters, and resolutions and also has the capability to manage photos. The S10 and the S10+ also come with a wide-angle lens and a telephoto lens.

» **Wireless email:** Send and receive email from your phone.

» **Multimedia:** Play music and videos on your phone.

» **Contact Manager:** The Galaxy S10 lets you take shortcuts that save you from having to enter someone's ten-digit number each time you want to call or text a friend. In fact, the Contact Manager can track all the numbers that an individual might have, store an email address and photo for the person, and synchronize with the program you use for managing contacts on both your personal and work PCs!

- **» Digital camcorder:** The Galaxy S10 comes with a built-in digital camcorder that records live video at a resolution that you can set, including 4K/UHD (ultra-high definition, which is the resolution that is available on the newest televisions).

- **» Mapping and directions:** The Galaxy S10 uses GPS (Global Positioning System) along with other complementary positioning systems to tell you where you are, find local services that you need, and give you directions to where you want to go.

- **» Fitness information:** The Galaxy S10 automatically tracks important health information within the phone and with external sensors.

- **» Business applications:** The Galaxy S10 can keep you productive while you're away from the office.

I go into each of these capabilities in greater detail in the following sections.

Internet access

Until a few years ago, the only way to access the Internet when you were away from a desk was with a laptop. Smartphones are a great alternative to laptops because they're small, convenient, and ready to launch their web browsers right away. Even more important, when you have a smartphone, you can access the Internet wherever you are — whether Wi-Fi is available or not.

The drawback to smartphones, however, is that their screen size is smaller than that of even the most basic laptop. On the Galaxy S10 phone, you can use the standard version of a website if you want. You can pinch and stretch your way to get the information you want. (See Chapter 2 for more information on pinching and stretching. For more information on accessing the Internet from your Galaxy S10 phone, turn to Chapter 7.)

To make things a bit easier, many popular websites offer an easier-to-use app that you can download and install on your phone. This is discussed in detail in Chapter 8. Essentially, the website reformats the information from the site so that it's easier to read and navigate in the mobile environment. Figure 1-1 compares a regular website with the app version of that website.

Full Web Page

Mobile App Home Page

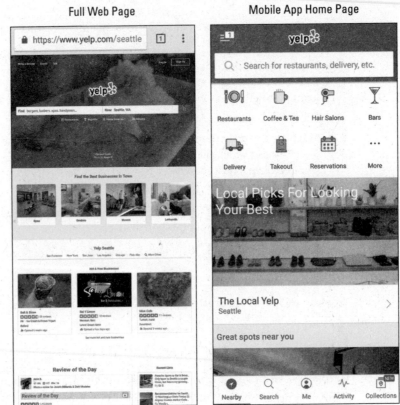

FIGURE 1-1:
A website and the
app version of
the main site.

Photos

The image application on your phone helps you use the digital camera on your
Galaxy S10 phone to its full potential. It would almost make sense to call the
Samsung Galaxy S10 a smart camera with a built-in phone! There are all kinds of
smarts in these applications that automatically figure out what you're trying to do
and make it so that you're suddenly the next Ansel Adams.

Studies have found that cellphone users tend to snap a bunch of pictures
within the first month of phone usage. After that, the photos sit on the phone
(instead of being downloaded to a computer), and the picture-taking rate drops
dramatically.

The Galaxy S10 image management application is different. You can integrate
your camera images into your home photo library, as well as photo-sharing sites
such as Google Photos and Instagram, with minimal effort.

For more on how to use the Photo applications, turn to Chapter 9.

Wireless email

On your Galaxy S10 smartphone, you can access your business and personal email accounts, reading and sending email messages on the go. Depending on your email system, you might be able to sync so that when you delete an email on your phone, the email is deleted on your computer at the same time so that you don't have to read the same messages on your phone and your computer.

Chapter 5 covers setting up your business and personal email accounts.

Multimedia

Some smartphones allow you to play music and videos on your phone. On the Galaxy S10, you can use the applications that come with the phone, or you can download applications that offer these capabilities from the Play Store.

Chapter 12 covers how to use the multimedia services with your Galaxy S10 phone.

An intelligent agent

Chapter 14 explores how to use Samsung's intelligent agent called Bixby. You simply ask Bixby to take care of things for you, such as update an appointment or check for prices and Bixby will go off and do it.

Customizing Your Phone with Games and Applications

Application developers — large and small — are working on the Android platform to offer a variety of applications and games for the Galaxy S10 phone. Compared to most of the other smartphone platforms, Google imposes fewer restrictions on application developers regarding what's allowable. This freedom to develop resonates with many developers — resulting in a bonanza of application development on this platform.

As of this writing, almost three million applications are available from Google's Play Store. For more information about downloading games and applications, turn to Chapter 8.

Downloading games

Chapter 10 of this book is for gamers. Although your phone comes with a few general-interest games, you can find a whole wide world of games for every skill and taste. In Chapter 10, I give you all the information you need to set up different gaming experiences. Whether you prefer stand-alone games or multiplayer games, you can set up your Galaxy S10 phone to get what you need.

Downloading applications

Your phone comes with some very nice applications, but these might not take you as far as you want to go. You might also have some special interests, such as philately or stargazing, that neither Samsung nor your carrier felt would be of sufficient general interest to include on the phone. (Can you imagine?)

Your phone also comes with preloaded *widgets*, which are smaller applications that serve particular purposes, such as retrieving particular stock quotes or telling you how your phone's battery is feeling today. Widgets reside on the extended Home screen and are instantly available.

Buying applications allows you to get additional capabilities quickly, easily, and inexpensively. Ultimately, these make your phone, which is already a reflection of who you are, even more personal as you add more capabilities.

TAKE A DEEP BREATH

You don't have to rush to implement every feature of your Galaxy S10 phone the very first day you get it. Instead, pick one capability at a time. Digest it, enjoy it, and then tackle the next one.

I recommend starting with setting up your email and social accounts, but that's just me.

No matter how you tackle the process of setting up your Galaxy S10 phone, it'll take some time. If you try to cram it all in on the first day, you'll turn what should be fun into drudgery.

The good news is that you own the book that takes you through the process. You can do a chapter or two at a time.

WHAT IF I DIDN'T GET MY PHONE FROM A CELLULAR COMPANY?

With a few exceptions, such as an "unlocked" GSM phone, each phone is associated with a particular cellular company. (In this context, a *locked* phone can work only on its original carrier.) Maybe you bought a secondhand phone on eBay, or you got a phone from a friend who didn't want his anymore. If you didn't get your phone directly from a cellular provider, you will need to figure out which provider the phone is associated with and get a service plan from that company.

If there's no logo on the front, you'll have to figure out which cellular carrier it can work with. The quickest way is to take the phone to any cellular store; the folks there know how to figure it out.

What's cool about the Android platform

The Samsung Galaxy S10 is a top-of-the-line Android phone. That means you can run any application developed for an Android phone to its full capability. This is significant because one of the founding principles behind the Android platform is to create an environment where application developers can be as creative as possible without an oppressive organization dictating what can and cannot be sold (as long as it's within the law, of course). This creative elbow room has inspired many of the best application developers to go with Android first.

In addition, Android is designed to run multiple applications at once. Other smartphone platforms have added this capability, but Android is designed to let you to jump quickly among the multiple apps that you're running — which makes your smartphone experience that much smoother.

Surviving Unboxing Day

When you turn on your phone the first time, it will ask you a series of ten questions and preferences to configure it. Frankly, they are trying to make this book unnecessary and put me out of business. The nerve!

The good folks at Samsung are well-intentioned, but not every customer who owns a Samsung Galaxy S10 knows, from day one, whether he or she wants a Samsung account, what's a good name for the phone, or what the purpose of a cloud service, such as Dropbox, is and how it would be used.

You can relax. I'll help you answer these questions — or, when appropriate, refer you to the chapter in this book that helps you come up with your answer.

On the other hand, if your phone is already set up, you probably took a guess or skipped some questions. Maybe now you're rethinking some of your choices. No problem. You can go back and change any answer you gave and get your phone to behave the way you want.

The following are the kinds of questions you may be asked. These questions may come in this order, but they may not. They typically include the following:

>> **Language/Accessibility:** This option lets you select your language. The default is English for phones sold within the United States. Also, the phone has some special capabilities for individuals with disabilities. If you have a disability and think you might benefit, take a look at these options. They have really tried to make this phone as usable as possible for as many folks as possible.

>> **Wi-Fi:** Your phone automatically starts scanning for a Wi-Fi connection. You can always use the cellular connection when you are in cellular coverage, but if there is a Wi-Fi connection available, your phone will try to use this first. It is probably cheaper and may be faster than the cellular.

At the same time, you may not want your phone to connect to the Wi-Fi access point with the best signal. It could be that the strongest signal is a fee-based service, whereas the next best signal is free. In any case, this page scans the available options and presents them to you.

>> **Date and Time:** This is easy. The default setting is to use the time and date that comes from the cellular network and the date and time format is the U.S. style. Just tap on the next button and move on. This date and time from the cellular network is the most accurate information you'll get, and you don't need to do anything other than be within cellular coverage now and again. If you prefer non-U.S. formatting, such as a 24-hour clock or day/month/year formatting, you can change your phone any way you want.

>> **Sign up for a Samsung Account:** Go ahead and sign up for an account. The Samsung account offers you some nice things to help you get your phone back should you lose it. All you need is an account name, such as an email account, and a password.

TIP

When you buy a Galaxy S10 smartphone, you are now a customer of multiple companies! These include Samsung for the phone hardware, Google for the phone operating system (Android), and the wireless carrier that provides the cellular service. Plus, if you bought the phone through a phone retailer, such as Best Buy, it is in the mix as well. All of them want to make you happy, which is a good thing for the most part. The only downside is that they want to know who you are so that they can provide you with more services. Don't worry. You control how much they offer you.

» **Google Account Sign-up:** *Google account* means an email account where the address ends in @gmail.com. If you already have an account on Gmail, enter your user ID and password here. If you don't have a Gmail account, I suggest waiting until you read Chapter 5. I highly recommend that you create a Gmail account, but there are some considerations on selecting a good name. If you are game, pick a name for your Gmail account now. Otherwise, it can wait until you read Chapter 5.

» **Location Options:** Your phone knowing your location and providing it to an application can be sensitive issue.

If you're really worried about privacy and security, tap the green check marks on the screen and then tap the button that says Next. Selecting these options prevents applications from knowing where you are. (This choice also prevents you from getting directions and a large number of cool capabilities that are built into applications.) The only folks who'll know your location will be the 911 dispatchers if you dial them.

If you're worried about your security but want to take advantage of some of the cool capabilities built into your phone, tap the right arrow key to move forward. Remember, you can choose on a case-by-case basis whether to share your location. (I cover this issue in Chapter 8.)

» **Phone Ownership:** This screen asks you to enter your first and last name. Go ahead and put in your real name. If you want to know more, read Chapter 5.

» **Cloud Services:** The chances are that you will be offered the option to sign up for a cloud service where you can back up your phone and get access to a gazillion MB of free storage. This can be a tricky decision. You could sign up for every cloud service that comes along. Then you need to remember where you stored that critical file. You could sign up for one, and you may miss a nice capability that is available on another. You could have one cloud service for work and another for personal. Here is what I recommend: Sign up for whatever is the cloud service your phone offers during this initial setup process if you do not already have one. You will see what it is later. If you are happy with a cloud service you already have, such as Dropbox or OneDrive, chances are, they will have all the services you need for you and your phone. You can link your Galaxy S10 to this service by downloading the necessary app (which I cover how to do in Chapter 8).

» **Learn about Key Features:** If you think you don't need this book, go ahead and take this tour of all the new things you can do. If you think you might need this book in any way, shape, or form, tap the Next button. This screen is for setting up the coolest and the most sophisticated capabilities of the phone. I cover many of them in this book. For now, skip this to get to the last screen.

>> **Device Name:** When this screen comes up, you'll see a text box that has the model name. You can keep this name for your phone, or you can choose to personalize it a bit. For example, you can change it to "Bill's Galaxy S10" or "Indy at 425-555-1234." The purpose of this name is for connecting to a local data network, as when you're pairing to a Bluetooth device. If this last sentence made no sense to you, don't worry about it. (I go over all of this in Chapter 3.) Tap Finish. In a moment, you see the Home screen, as shown in Figure 1-2.

FIGURE 1-2:
The Home screen
for the Samsung
Galaxy S10.

Chapter **2**

Beginning at the Beginning

n this chapter, I fill you in on the basics of using your new Samsung Galaxy S10. You start by turning on your phone. (I told you I was covering the basics!) I guide you through charging your phone and getting the most out of your phone's battery. Stick with me for a basic tour of your phone's buttons and other features. Then I end by telling you how to turn off your phone or put it in "sleep" mode.

TIP

Unless you're new to mobile phones in general — and smartphones in particular — you might want to skip this chapter. If the term "smartphone" is foreign to you, you probably haven't used one before, and reading this chapter won't hurt. And, just so you know, a *smartphone* is just a mobile phone on which you can download and run applications that are better than what comes preloaded on a phone right out of the box.

First Things First: Turning On Your Phone

When you open the box of your new phone, the packaging will present you with your phone, wrapped in plastic, readily accessible. If you haven't already, take the phone out of the box and remove any protective covering material on the screen. (There is no need to keep the plastic. It is not an effective screen protector!)

First things first. The Power button is on the right side of the phone. You can see where in Figure 2-1. Press the Power button for a second and see whether it vibrates and the screen lights up. Hopefully, your phone arrived with enough electrical charge that you won't have to plug it into an outlet right away. You can enjoy your new phone for the first day without having to charge it.

FIGURE 2-1:
The Power button on the Galaxy S10.

The phones that you get at the stores of most cellular carriers usually come with the battery partially charged and registered with the network.

REMEMBER

If the screen does light up, don't hold the Power button too long, or the phone might turn off.

If the phone screen doesn't light up (rats!), you need to charge the battery. That means that you have to wait to use your beautiful new phone. Sorry.

THE NITTY-GRITTY OF HOW YOUR PHONE WORKS

TECHNICAL STUFF

As soon as you turn on your phone, several things happen. As the phone is powering up, it begins transmitting information to (and receiving information from) nearby cellular towers. The first information exchanged includes your phone's electronic serial number. Every cellphone has its own unique serial number built into the hardware of the phone; the serial number in current-generation cellphones can't be duplicated or used by any other phone.

This electronic serial number is also called an International Mobile Equipment Identity (IMEI) number. It is 14 or 15 digits long. Cellular equipment is fine with long numbers. We mere mortals have enough trouble remembering 10-digit numbers, even with the hack of having only a limited number of area codes. To help us out, you and I get to use the shorter number and the cellular equipment happily keeps track of the 10-digit and the 14/15-digit numbers and shows us only what we can handle.

It doesn't matter to the phone or the cellular tower if you're near your home when you turn on your phone — and that's the joy of mobile phones. All cellular networks have agreements that allow you to use cellular networks in other parts of the country and, sometimes, around the world.

That said, a call outside your cellular provider's own network may be expensive. Within the United States, many service plans allow you to pay the same rate if you use your phone anywhere in the United States to call anywhere in the United States. If you travel outside the United States, even to Canada, you might end up paying through the nose. *Remember:* Before you leave on a trip, check with your cellular carrier about your rates. Even if you travel internationally only a few times yearly, a different service plan may work better for you. Your cellular carrier can fill you in on your options.

Charging Your Phone and Managing Battery Life

In the package when you buy your phone, you find a two-piece battery charger (cable and the transformer), as shown in Figure 2-2.

FIGURE 2-2:
The transformer
and USB cable for
charging your
phone.

Wall Charger   USB-A/USB-C Cable

The cable has two ends: one end that plugs into the phone, and the other that's a standard rectangular USB connector. The phone end is a small connector called a *USB-C* that is used on many Samsung devices and is the standard for charging cellphones and other small electronics — and for connecting them to computers.

TIP

One cool thing you will notice about the USB-C connector is that you can insert it either side up. The older, rectangular USB-A connector probably drove you crazy because it wouldn't go in if you had the plug upside down. You still have that problem with the wall charger and cable, but you won't have the problem with the cable and phone!

To charge the phone, you have two choices:

>> Plug the transformer into a wall socket and then plug the cable's USB plug into the USB receptacle in the transformer. This is the option I recommend.

>> Plug the USB on the cable into a USB port on your PC.

Then you plug the small end of the cable into the phone. The port is on the bottom of the phone. Make sure that you push the little metal plug all the way in.

REMEMBER

It doesn't really matter in what order you plug in things. However, if you use the USB port on a PC, the PC needs to be powered on for the phone to charge.

TIP

Your phone will charge faster with a Samsung wall charger that has Adaptive Fast Charging on it. When the wall charger, or car charger has Adaptive Fast Charging, it knows if the phone is getting too warm and slow down the speed of charging. Because the charging speed can slow down, it can go faster the rest of the time.

If your phone is off when you're charging the battery, an image of a battery appears onscreen for a moment. The green portion of the battery indicates the amount of charge within the battery. You can get the image to reappear with a quick press of the Power button. This image tells you the status of the battery without your having to turn on the phone.

If your phone is on, you see a small battery icon at the top of the screen showing how much charge is in the phone's battery. When the battery in the phone is fully charged, it vibrates to let you know that it's done charging.

Depending upon the circumstances, it can take less than an hour to go from a dead battery to a fully charged battery. You don't need to wait for the battery to be fully charged. You can partially recharge and run if you want.

TIP

You'll hear all kinds of "battery lore" left over from earlier battery technologies. For example, lithium-ion (Li-ion) batteries in your S10 don't have a "memory" (a bad thing for a battery) as nickel-cadmium (NiCad) batteries did. That means that you don't have to make sure that the battery fully discharges before you recharge it. In fact, you want to avoid fully discharging the battery if you can avoid it.

In addition to the transformer and USB cable that come with the phone, you have other optional charging tools:

>> **USB travel charger:** If you already have a USB travel charger, you can leave the transformer at home. This accessory will run you about $15. You still need your cable, although any USB-to-USB-C cable should work.

>> **Car charger:** You can buy a charger with a USB port that plugs into the power socket/cigarette lighter in a car. This is convenient if you spend a lot of time in your car. The list price is $30, but you can get the real Samsung car charger for less at some online stores.

>> **Portable external charger:** You can buy a portable external charger that you can use to recharge your phone without having to plug into the power socket or cigarette lighter in a car. You charge this gizmo before your travel and connect it only when the charge in your phone starts to get low. These usually involve re-chargeable batteries, but some of these products use photovoltaic cells to transform light into power. As long as there is a USB port (the female part of the USB), all you need is your cable. These chargers can cost from $30 to $100 on up. See some options in Figure 2-3.

FIGURE 2-3:
Some portable
external charging
options.

Images courtesy of myCharge

>> **Wireless charger:** This option is slick. You simply put your phone on a charging mat or in a cradle, and the phone battery will start charging! Your Galaxy S10 uses the widely adopted Qi standard (pronounced *chee*). This option saves you from having to plug and unplug your phone.

WARNING

Ideally, use Samsung chargers or chargers from reputable manufacturers or retailers. The power specifications for USB ports are standardized. Reputable manufactures comply with these standards, but less reputable manufacturers might not. Cheap USB chargers physically fit the USB end of the cable that goes to your phone. However, Li-ion batteries are sensitive to voltage. There are many, many creative options available outside the store where you bought your phone, but avoid the allure of low price.

WARNING

Be aware that the conditions that make for a good charge with a photocell also tend to make for high heat. It will do you little good to have a beautifully functioning charger and a dead phone.

Most of the chargers out there are either for the Apple iPhone and have an Apple Lightning connector or have a micro-USB connector. As you know, your phone has a USB-C connector. A micro USB will not work with a USB-C connector. You either need to get a cable that has a USB-C connector or use an adapter that will allow you to connect micro USB to a USB-C connector. Figure 2-4 shows the micro USB to USB-C adapter next to a dime for a size comparison.

FIGURE 2-4:
The micro USB to
USB-C adapter.

ONLY YOU CAN PREVENT PHONE FIRES

**TECHNICAL
STUFF**

The Galaxy S10 uses lithium-ion (Li-ion) batteries. As the name implies, these batteries are based upon the element lithium (Li). Lithium works really well for cellphone batteries because it's very light.

The problem is that if lithium gets too hot, it burns. Lithium can catch fire at a relatively modest 180°F, and then burn like crazy at 1,100°F. By comparison, dry firewood won't ignite until 451°F, and will then burn at 1,100°F. In other words, lithium burns just as hot as a campfire, but it ignites at a much lower temperature.

To make things safe, battery makers and cellphone manufacturers implement all kinds of sneaky and imaginative methods of removing the heat from around the lithium battery. In addition, your phone invisibly monitors temperatures and takes steps to ensure that it doesn't get too hot. This all works so well and seamlessly that you probably didn't even notice this was happening in your earlier phones and other gizmos that use Li-ion technology.

So, here's the big problem: If things start going wrong with Lithium-ion batteries, many of the sneaky and imaginative methods used to remove the heat begin to fail. The fancy term for what happens next is *thermal runaway.* When thermal runaway happens in a device with a Li-ion battery, one of two things happens:

- The guts of the phone will bubble and melt.
- The battery will burst into flames, throwing sparks for several feet in all directions.

So, what should you do and, perhaps more important, what should you *not* do? If your phone has started to burn, the best possible solution is to dunk it in a glass, bucket, or toilet full of water. If you can't find something to dunk it in, you can throw water on the phone to stop the fire. Water both cools the lithium and prevents oxygen from getting to the flame. I know: Getting your phone wet goes against all your instincts, but once a

(continued)

(continued)

phone has started bubbling, all your texts and photos have already been lost. Prevent further damage and use water to put out the fire.

If you don't have water handy, and you're somewhere outside, in a parking lot or on a sidewalk away from people, you can set the phone on the ground, get far away from it, and call 911. Stand far back from the phone. It could explode. For obvious reasons, putting out the fire by dunking the phone in water or dousing it with water is best.

Smothering the phone with a blanket or dirt won't work. Even if you get the fire stopped momentarily with these methods, the battery is likely to start burning again because it's still too hot. A fire extinguisher with anything other than water or a liquid will also not work well. As with a blanket or dirt, the battery stays hot, and when oxygen reaches it, the lithium will simply reignite.

INCREASING YOUR CHARGING KNOWLEDGE

There are so many charging options out there these days, it can be confusing. My simple advice is to use a USB-C cable from Samsung that has Adaptive Fast Charging. The next best choice is a name-brand charger that has USB-C. Some well-meaning "friends" may try to lead you astray and try something else. Do not allow yourself to be fooled.

The following figure shows some of the options that are out in the market right now. The USB-C is on the left. The ones to the right will not work with your phone. Buying these would be a waste of money unless you plan to use the adapter. Otherwise, these won't fit in the receptacle on your phone.

Enlarged Connector Front View

Connector Side View

Micro-USB C Type Connector

Micro-USB Connector

Micro-USB 3.0 Connector

Apple Lightning™ Connector

The first option is the micro-USB. This is what is used on the Galaxy S6, the S7, and many phones from other manufacturers.

The second option is the micro-USB 3.0. The front view of the micro-USB 3.0 connector looks like the micro-USB connector front view with a rectangle welded on to the right. Frankly, it kinda looks silly, which is why it never really caught on. Samsung used it on the Galaxy S5, which is why you might see it in some stores.

The third option is the Apple Lighting cable. This is unlike the others because the connectors are visible rather than being protected by a metal shroud. The best thing about it is that it costs more, as you can see in the figure that shows car charges from Ventev (one of those reputable suppliers I have told you about).

Ventev dashport r2340c charger with Micro USB Cable $29.99

Ventev dashport r2340c charger w/ Apple Lightning™ Cable $34.99

Images courtesy of Ventev

The same product has a $5 premium for the Apple connector.

SHARING IS CARING: WIRELESS POWERSHARE

A great deal of attention is paid to keeping your phone charged. Sometimes your phone has plenty of power, but another device is running low. Your S10 has a cool new feature called Wireless PowerShare. You go into Settings, turn this capability on, and the back of your S10 becomes a wireless charger! You can charge the Galaxy S9 of your best friend and be a hero for the day.

Navigating the Galaxy S10

Galaxy S10 phone devices differ from many other mobile phones in design: They have significantly fewer hardware buttons (physical buttons on the phone). They rely much more heavily on software buttons that appear onscreen.

In this section, I guide you through your phone's buttons.

The phone's hardware buttons

Samsung has reduced the number of hardware buttons on the Galaxy S10. There are only three: the Power button, the Volume button, and the Bixby button. Before you get too far into using your phone, orient yourself to be sure that you're looking at the correct side of the phone. When I refer to the *left* or *right* of the phone, I'm assuming a vertical orientation (meaning you're not holding the phone sideways) and that you're looking at the phone's screen.

The Power button

The Power button (refer to Figure 2-1) is on right side of the phone, toward the top when you hold it in vertical orientation.

In addition to powering up the phone, pressing the Power button puts the device into sleep mode if you press it for a moment while the phone is On. *Sleep mode* shuts off the screen and suspends most running applications.

The phone automatically goes into sleep mode after about 30 seconds of inactivity to save power, but you might want to do this manually when you put away your phone. The Super AMOLED (Active-Matrix Organic Light-Emitting Diode) screen on your Samsung Galaxy S10 is cool, but it also uses a lot of power.

REMEMBER

Don't confuse sleep mode with powering off. Because the screen is the biggest user of power on your phone, having the screen go blank saves battery life. The phone is still alert to any incoming calls; when someone calls, the screen automatically lights up.

The Volume button(s)

Technically, there are two Volume buttons: one to increase the volume, and the other to lower it. Their locations are shown in Figure 2-5.

Bixby button

Volume button

FIGURE 2-5:
The Galaxy S10
Volume buttons
on the left.

The Volume buttons control the volume of all the audio sources on the phone, including:

» The phone ringer for when a call comes in (ringtone).

» The notifications that occur only when you're not talking on the phone, such as the optional ping that lets you know you've received a text or email.

» The phone headset when you're talking on the phone.

» The volume from the digital music and video player (media).

The volume controls are aware of the context; they can tell which volume you're changing. For example, if you're listening to music, adjusting volume raises or lowers the music volume, but leaves the ringer and phone-earpiece volumes unchanged.

The Volume buttons are complementary to software settings you can make within the applications. For example, you can open the music-player software and turn up the volume on the appropriate screen. Then you can use the hardware buttons to turn down the volume, and you'll see the volume setting on the screen go down.

Another option is to go to a settings screen and set the volume levels for each scenario. Here's how to do that:

1. **From the Home screen, press either Volume button.**

   You can press it either up or down. Doing so brings up the screen shown in Figure 2-6.

   If you press the volume up or down, the ring tone gets louder or softer. Hold off on this tweak for now and go to the next step.

FIGURE 2-6:
The ringer
volume pop-up.

2. **From this screen, tap the arrow down in the upper-right corner.**

   Tapping it brings up the screen shown in Figure 2-7.

3. **From the screen shown in Figure 2-7, set the volume at the desired setting.**

   You can adjust the volume of any setting by placing your finger on the dot on the slider image. The dot will get bigger; you can slide it to the left to lower this particular volume setting or to the right to raise it.

FIGURE 2-7:
The All Volume
Settings pop-up.

The Bixby button

The Bixby button on the phone is shown in Figure 2-5. It's below the volume buttons. Bixby is an app from Samsung that is an *intelligent agent* (IA). It's like Alexa or Siri on the iPhone. I cover Bixby in greater detail in Chapter 14. It's cool — and they keep adding new capabilities. The plan is that you can launch this app by pressing the Bixby button twice. For now, it will bring you to the Bixby screen.

The touchscreen

To cram all the information that you need onto one screen, Samsung takes the modern approach to screen layout. You'll want to become familiar with several finger-navigation motions used to work with your screen.

Before diving in, though, here's a small list of terms you need to know:

>> **Icon:** An *icon* is a little image. Tapping an icon launches an application or performs some function, such as making a telephone call.

>> **Button:** A *button* on a touchscreen is meant to look like a three-dimensional button that you would push on, say, a telephone. Buttons are typically labeled to tell you what they do when you tap them. For example, you'll see buttons labeled Save or Send.

>> **Hyperlink:** Sometimes called a *link* for short, a *hyperlink* is text that performs some function when you tap it. Usually text is lifeless. If you tap a word and it does nothing, then it's just text. If you tap a word and it launches a website or causes a screen to pop up, it's a hyperlink.

>> **Thumbnail:** A *thumbnail* is a small, low-resolution version of a larger, high-resolution picture stored somewhere else.

With this background, it's time to discuss the motions you'll be using on the touchscreen.

WARNING

You need to clean the touchscreen glass from time to time. The glass on your phone is Gorilla Glass (made by Corning) — the toughest stuff available to protect against breakage. Use a soft cloth or microfiber to get fingerprints off. You can even wipe the touchscreen on your clothes. However, never use a paper towel! Over time, glass is no match for the fibers in the humble paper towel.

Tap

Often, you just tap the screen to make things happen (as when you launch an app) or select options. Think of a *tap* as a single mouse click on a computer screen.

A tap is simply a touch on the screen, much like using a touchscreen at a retail kiosk. Figure 2-8 shows what the tap motion should look like.

FIGURE 2-8:
The tap motion.

One difference between a mouse click on a computer and a tap on a Galaxy S10 phone is that a single tap launches applications on the phone in the same way that a double-click of the mouse launches an application on a computer.

TIP

A tap is different from press and hold (see the next section). If you leave your finger on the screen for more than an instant, the phone thinks you want to do something other than launch an application.

Press and hold

Press and hold, as the name implies, involves putting your finger on an icon on the screen and leaving it there for more than a second. What happens when you leave your finger on an icon depends upon the situation.

For example, when you press and hold on an application on the Home screen (the screen that comes up after you turn on the phone), a garbage-can icon appears onscreen. This is to remove that icon from that screen. And when you press and hold an application icon from the list of applications, the phone assumes that you want to copy that application to your Home screen. Don't worry if these distinctions might not make sense yet. The point is that you should be familiar with holding and pressing — and that it's different from tapping.

You don't need to tap or press and hold very hard for the phone to know that you want it to do something. Neither do you need to worry about breaking the glass, even by pressing on it very hard. If you hold the phone in one hand and tap with the other, you'll be fine. I suppose you might break the glass on the phone if you put it on the floor and press up into a one-fingered handstand. I don't recommend that, but if you do try it, please post the video on YouTube.

On average, a person calls 911 about once every year. Usually, you call 911 because of a stressful situation. Like every phone, the Samsung Galaxy S10 has a special stress sensor that causes it to lock up when you need it most. Okay, not really, but it seems that way. When you're stressed, it's easy to think that you're tapping when you're actually pressing and holding. Be aware of this tendency and remember to *tap*.

Moving around the screen or to the next screen

Additional finger motions help you move around the screens and to adjust the scaling for images that you want on the screen. Mastering these motions is important to getting the most from your phone.

The first step is navigating the screen to access what's not visible onscreen. Think of this as navigating a regular computer screen, where you use a horizontal scroll bar to access information to the right or left of what's visible on your monitor, or a vertical scroll bar to move you up and down on a screen.

The same concept works on your phone. To overcome the practical realities of screen size on a phone that will fit into your pocket, the Galaxy S10 phone uses a *panorama* screen layout, meaning that you keep scrolling left or right (or maybe up and down) to access different screens.

In a nutshell, although the full width of a screen is accessible, only the part bounded by the physical screen of the Galaxy S10 phone is visible on the display. Depending upon the circumstances, you have several ways to get to information not visible on the active screen. These actions include drag, flicks, pinch and stretch, and double taps. I cover all these gestures in the following sections.

Drag

The simplest finger motion on the phone is the *drag*. You place your finger on a point on the screen and then drag the image with your finger. Then you lift your finger. Figure 2-9 shows what the motion looks like.

FIGURE 2-9:
The drag motion
for controlled
movement.

Dragging allows you to move slowly around the panorama. This motion is like clicking a scroll bar and moving it slowly.

Flick

To move quickly around the panorama, you can *flick* the screen to move in the direction of your flick (see Figure 2-10).

FIGURE 2-10:
Use a flick motion
for faster
movement.

Better control of this motion comes with practice. In general, the faster the flick, the more the panorama moves. However, some screens (such as the extended Home screen) move only one screen to the right or left, no matter how fast you flick.

Pinch and stretch

Some screens allow you to change the scale of images you view on your screen. When this feature is active, the Zoom options change the magnification of the area on the screen. You can zoom out to see more features at a smaller size or zoom in to see more detail at a larger size.

To zoom out, you put two fingers (apart) on the screen and pull them together to pinch the image. Make sure you're centered on the spot that you want to see in more detail. The pinch motion is shows in Figure 2-11.

FIGURE 2-11:
Use the pinch
motion to
zoom out.

The opposite motion is to zoom in. This involves the stretch motion, as shown in Figure 2-12. You place two fingers (close together) and stretch them apart.

FIGURE 2-12:
Use the stretch
motion to
zoom in.

Double tap

The *double tap* (shown in Figure 2-13) just means tapping the same button area on the screen twice in rapid succession. You use the double tap to jump between a zoomed-in and a zoomed-out image to get you back to the previous resolution. This option saves you frustration in getting back to a familiar perspective.

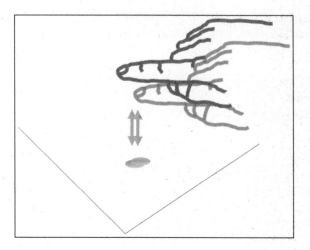

FIGURE 2-13:
The double-tap
motion.

REMEMBER

When you double tap, time the taps so that the phone doesn't interpret them as two separate taps. With a little practice, you'll master the timing of the second tap.

The extended Home screen

The Home screen is the first screen you see when the phone is done with setting up. Additional screens off to the right and left. make up the extended Home screen. They can be seen as a panorama in Figure 2-14.

Home Screen

At any given moment, you see only one screen at a time. You navigate among the screen by flicking to the right and left. The Home button, which we describe in more detail in the next section, will always bring you back to the Home screen.

The extended Home screen is where you can organize icons and other functions to best make the phone convenient for you. Out of the box, Samsung and your cellular carrier have worked together to create a starting point for you. Beyond that, though, you have lots of ways you can customize your Home screens for easy access to the things that are most important to you. Much of the book covers all the things that the phone can do, but a recurring theme is how to put your favorite capabilities on your Home screen, if you wish.

To start, check out the layout of the Home screen and how it relates to other areas of the phone. Knowing these areas is important for basic navigation.

Figure 2-15 shows a typical Home screen and highlights three important areas on the phone:

» **The notification area:** This part of the screen presents you with small icons that let you know if something important is up, like battery life or a coupon from McDonald's.

» **The primary shortcuts:** These four icons remain stationary as you move across the Home screen. If you notice in Figure 2-15, these have been determined by Samsung and your cellular carrier to be the four most important applications on your phone and are on all the screens.

» **The Function keys:** These three keys control essential phone functions, regardless of what else is going on at the moment with the phone.

Notification area

App Shortcuts

Google Search Engine with Voice Recognition

Primary Shortcuts

Function Keys

FIGURE 2-15: Important areas on the Galaxy S10 phone and Home screen.

There are a series of dots just above the primary shortcuts on the extended Home screen. You may also notice that one of the dots isn't just a dot — it's a little house. That is the "home" Home screen. The brightest dot indicates where you are among the screens. You can navigate among screens by dragging the screen to the left or right. This moves you one screen at a time. You can also jump multiple screens by tapping on the dot that corresponds to the screen number you want to see or by dragging the dots to the screen you want to see. The following sections give you more detail on each area.

Using the Home button

One of the important design features Samsung has implemented with the Galaxy phone is the "invisible" Home button. Some other smartphones have a physical button on the bottom of the front screen. To offer more screen real estate, the S10 makes it a software-based button on the bottom in the center of the function keys.

The Home button (see Figure 2-16) may not look like much, but it is very important because it brings you back to the Home screen from wherever you are in an application. If you're working on applications and feel like you're helplessly lost, don't worry. Press the Home button, close your eyes, click your heels together three times, and think to yourself, "There's no place like home," and you will be brought back to the Home screen.

FIGURE 2-16:
The Galaxy S10
Home button on
the front.

Home button

You don't really need to do all that other stuff after pressing the Home button. Just pressing the Home button does the trick.

Adding shortcuts to the Home screen

You have a lot of screen real estate where you can put icons of your favorite applications and widgets (refer to Figure 2-14). (*Widgets* are small apps that take care of simple functions, like displaying time or the status of your battery.) You can add shortcuts to the apps and to these widgets to your Home screen by following these steps:

1. **From the extended Home screen page where there is some space for the icon of an app, swipe your finger upward on the screen.**

   This brings up a directory of all the apps you currently have on the phone. The number of apps and pages for their icons is practically unlimited. (I cover how to add new apps in Chapter 8.)

2. **Press and hold the icon of the app you want to add.**

   The icon under your finger will get a pop-up like the one shown in in Figure 2-17.

FIGURE 2-17:
An Apps page.

3. **Tap the Add to Home option.**

   The icon now appears in a random spot on one of your home pages. If you like where the icon is, you're all set. If you want to move it to another spot on your Home page, continue on to the next step.

4. **Press and hold the icon you want to move.**

   Two things happen with the icon. First you get a pop-up that asks you if you want to uninstall the app and some other options. To move the icon, slide your finger on the screen to where you want it to live. When you're happy with its location, lift your finger and it now has a new home.

Done.

Taking away shortcuts

Say that you find that you really don't use that app as much as you thought you would, and you want to have less clutter on your Home page. No problem. Press and hold the icon. A pop-up like the one shown in Figure 2-18 appears.

FIGURE 2-18:
The shortcut
pop-up on the
Home page.

Simply tap the garbage can, and off it goes to its maker.

It's gone from your Home page, but if you made a mistake, you can get it back easily enough. To re-create it, simply go back to the App Menu key and follow the process again. It's still on your phone.

The notification area and screen

The notification area is located at the top of the phone (refer to Figure 2-15). Here, you see little status icons. Maybe you received a text or an email, or you'll see an application needs some tending to.

Think of the notification area as a special email inbox where your carrier (or even the phone itself) can give you important information about what's happening with your phone. These little icons at the top tell you the condition of the different radio systems on your phone: The number of bars shown gives you an indication of signal strength, and usually the phone will also tell you what kind of mobile data speed you're getting — such as 3G or 4G.

You could take the time to learn the meanings of all the little icons that might come up, but that would take you a while. A more convenient option is to touch the notification area and pull it down, as shown in Figure 2-19.

The rest of the screen is written so that you can understand what's going on and what, if anything, you're expected to do — for example, if you see that you have connected to the Wi-Fi access point you intended.

When you're finished reading the notifications, you slide your finger back up to the top. If this screen gets too full, you can clear it by tapping the Clear button. You can also clear notifications one at a time by touching each one and swiping it to the side.

If you want a shortcut to control some key phone capabilities, you can tap one of these icons. For example, if you want to turn off Wi-Fi, you could just tap the Wi-Fi icon. This would save you from having to get in to Settings to do the same thing.

Notification Area Options

FIGURE 2-19:
Notification area
pull-down.

If you want to add more of these, simply tap the three vertical dots highlighted in Figure 2-19 to see your notification area options. These are seen in Figure 2-20, although you may have slightly different choices on your phone.

Button grid

3X3   4X3   5X3

OK

FIGURE 2-20:
Notification area
options.

For example, many people find the Flashlight capability to be handy. If it is not already there when you pull down the notifications screen, see whether it is among the options. If it is, press and hold on the flashlight icon. Then drag it to the top. The other icons scatter, and then you release it. You turn on the flashlight by tapping it. Try it and see.

The Device Function keys

At the bottom of the screen are three important buttons: the Device Function keys. They're always ready for you to navigate your phone even though they might switch off to hide their presence and give you more screen. Whatever else you're doing on the phone, these buttons can take over. I talk about the Home button earlier in this chapter. The other buttons are equally cool.

Recent Apps button

The button to the left of the Home button, the three vertical lines, is the Recent Apps button. Tapping the button brings up a list of the open apps. This is handy to navigate between running apps. Figure 2-21 shows a typical screen of recent apps.

FIGURE 2-21:
Recent Apps
screen.

You can scroll among the open apps by flicking left or right. You can jump to one of these apps by tapping somewhere on the image. You can also shut down one of the apps by flicking upward. You can shut them all down by tapping the link at the bottom that says Close All.

The Device Function keys are cool because they light up when you're touching them or the screen, but fade away the rest of the time.

The Back button

The Back button on your phone is similar to the Back button in a web browser: It takes you back one screen.

As you start navigating through the screens on your phone, tapping the Back button takes you back to the previous screen. If you keep tapping the Back button, you'll eventually return to the Home screen.

The keyboard

The screen of the Galaxy S10 phone is important, but you'll still probably spend more time on the keyboard entering data on the QWERTY keyboard.

Using the software keyboard

The software keyboard automatically pops up when the application detects a need for user text input. The keyboard, shown in Figure 2-22, appears at the bottom of the screen.

FIGURE 2-22:
Use the software keyboard to enter data.

Using voice recognition

The third option for a keyboard is . . . no keyboard at all! Galaxy S10 phones come with voice recognition as an option. It's very easy and works surprisingly well. In most spots where you have an option to enter text, you see a small version of the microphone icon shown in Figure 2-23.

Just tap this icon and say what you would have typed. You see the phone thinking for a second, and then a screen tells you that it is listening. Go ahead and start talking. When you're done, you can tap the Done button or just be quiet and wait. Within a few seconds, you'll read what you just said!

The orientation of the phone

Earlier in this chapter where I discuss the Power button, I refer to the phone being in vertical orientation (so that the phone is tall and narrow). It can also be used in the *landscape* orientation (sideways, or so that the phone is short and wide). The phone senses in which direction you're holding it and orients the screen to make it easier for you to view.

REMEMBER

The phone makes its orientation known to the application, but not all applications are designed to change their inherent display. That nuance is left to the writers of the application. For example, your phone can play videos. However, the video player application that comes with your phone shows video in landscape mode only.

In addition, the phone can sense when you're holding it to your ear. When it senses that it's held in this position, it shuts off the screen. You need not be concerned that you'll accidentally "chin-dial" a number in Botswana.

Going to Sleep Mode/Turning Off the Phone

You can leave your phone on every minute until you're ready to upgrade to the newest Galaxy S10 phone in a few years, but that would use up your battery in no time. Instead, put your idle phone in sleep mode to save battery power. *Note:* Your phone goes into sleep mode automatically after 30 seconds of inactivity on the screen.

TIP

You can adjust the sleep time out for a longer duration, which I cover in Chapter 16. Or you can manually put the phone in sleep mode by pressing the Power button for just a moment.

Sometimes it's best to simply shut down the phone if you aren't going to use it for several days or more. To shut down the phone completely, simply press and hold the Power button for a few seconds. The following options appear:

>> **Power Off:** Shut down the phone completely.

>> **Restart:** The Android operating system is stable. Well, mostly stable. Sometimes you may want to reboot it because it starts acting quirky. Tap the restart option and see whether that solves the problem.

>> **Emergency Mode:** This is an interesting option. Once you have agreed to some terms and conditions, your phone will go into hibernation, but it can come back to life quickly if you feel you need to dial 911. Before you can use this option, you need to agree to some of the limitations.

Good night!

2
Communicating with Other People

Chapter **3**

Calling People

At its essence, any cellphone — no matter how fancy or smart — exists to make phone calls. The good news is that making and receiving phone calls on your Galaxy S10 is easy.

In this chapter, I show you not only how to make a call, but also how to use your call list to keep track of your calls. And don't skip the section on using your phone for emergencies.

Finally, if you're like many people, you're never doing just one thing at a time, and a Bluetooth headset can make it easier for you to talk on the phone while driving and getting directions, checking email, wrangling kids and dogs, or just plain living life. In this chapter, I show you how to hook up your phone to a Bluetooth headset so that you can make and receive phone calls hands-free.

Making Calls

After your phone is on and you're connected to your cellular carrier (see Chapters 1 and 2), you can make a phone call. It all starts from the Home screen. Along the bottom of the screen, above the Device Function keys, are either four or five icons, which are the *primary shortcuts* (see Figure 3-1). The primary shortcuts on your phone may differ slightly, but in this case, from left to right, they are

>> Phone

>> Camera

>> Email

>> Messages

FIGURE 3-1:
The primary
shortcuts on the
Home screen.

To make a call, follow these steps:

1. **From the Home screen, tap the Phone icon.**

   You will see a screen like the one shown in Figure 3-2. This screen, called Recents, shows any calls you have made or received, such as the one from your carrier to confirm that you phone has been set up correctly.

2. **Tap the Keypad link at the bottom left of your screen.**

   This icon is a green circle with little white dots that symbolize the touch pad on a regular landline phone.

3. **Tap the telephone number you want to call.**

   The Keypad screen (see Figure 3-3) appears. This looks like a full-sized version of a touch pad on a regular landline phone.

   TIP

   For long distance calls while in the United States, you don't need to dial 1 before the area code — just dial the area code and then the seven-digit phone number. Similarly, you can include the 1 and the area code for local calls. On the other hand, if you're traveling internationally, you need to include the 1 — and be prepared for international roaming charges!

   In Chapter 6, you can read about how to make a phone call through your contacts.

FIGURE 3-2:
The Main screen
for the phone.

Keypad Icon

4. **Tap the green phone button at the bottom of the screen to place the call.**

   The screen changes to the screen shown in Figure 3-4. You have a chance to verify you dialed the person you intended.

   Within a few seconds, you should hear the phone ringing at the other end or a busy signal. From then on, it is like a regular phone call.

5. **When you're done with your call, tap the red phone button at the bottom of the screen.**

   The call is disconnected.

Without Telephone Number

With Telephone Number

FIGURE 3-3:
Dial the number from the Keypad screen.

If the other party answers the phone, you have a few options available to you by tapping on the correct icon/hyperlink on the screen, including:

>> Put the call on hold.

>> Add another call to have a three-way conversation.

>> Increase the volume.

>> Switch on a Bluetooth device (see the section "Syncing a Bluetooth Headset," later in this chapter).

>> Turn on the phone's speaker.

>> Bring up the keypad to enter numbers.

>> Mute the microphone on the phone.

You can do any or all of these, or you can just enjoy talking on the phone.

FIGURE 3-4:
Dialing screen.

If the call doesn't go through, either the cellular coverage where you are is insufficient, or your phone got switched to Airplane mode, which shuts off all the radios in the phone. (It's possible, of course, that your cellular carrier let you out the door without having set you up for service, but that's pretty unlikely!)

Check the notification section at the top of the screen. If there are no connection-strength bars, try moving to another location. If you see a small airplane silhouette, bring down the notification screen (see how in Chapter 2) and tap the plane icon to turn off Airplane mode.

TIP

If you pull down the notification screen and you don't see the green silhouette of an airplane, scroll the green or gray icons to the left. This icon may be off the page. Alternatively, tap the icon with the boxes in the upper-right corner, and you will see all the notification icons.

Answering Calls

Receiving a call is even easier than making a call. When someone calls you, caller ID information appears in a pop-up screen. Figure 3-5 shows some screen options for an incoming call.

Full Screen Incoming call   Partial Screen Incoming call

FIGURE 3-5:
Possible screens
when you're
receiving a call.

If you aren't doing anything with the phone at that moment, it will present you with the full screen. If you're using an app, it will give you a pop-up screen, as shown in the image on the right. To answer the call, tap or slide the green phone button. To not answer a call, you can simply ignore the ringing, or you can tap or slide the red phone button. The ringing stops immediately, and in either case, the call goes to voicemail.

In Part 4, I fill you in on some exciting options that you can enable (or not) when you get a call. For example, you can specify a unique ringtone for a particular number, or have an image of the caller pop up (if you save your contacts to your phone).

TIP

Regardless of what you were doing on the phone at that moment — such as listening to music or playing a game — the answer pop-up screen can appear. Any active application, including music or video, is suspended until the call is over.

REMEMBER

For callers to leave you messages, you must set up your voicemail. If you haven't yet set up your voicemail, the caller will hear a recorded message saying that your voicemail account isn't yet set up. Some cellular carriers can set up voicemail for you when you activate the account and get the phone; others require you to set up voicemail on your own. Ask how voicemail works at your carrier store or look for instructions in the manual included with your phone.

The answer and reject icons are pretty standard on any cellular phone. However, your Galaxy S10 is no standard phone. There is a third option, and what happens depends on your individual phone. In addition to the standard options of answer or reject, you have one more option — to reject *and* send the caller a text message. As your caller is sent to your voicemail, you also can immediately send the caller a text message that acknowledges the call.

Some of the typical canned messages that you can send are:

>> Sorry, I'm busy. Call back later.

>> I'm in a meeting.

>> I'll call you back.

>> I'm at the movie theater.

>> I'm in class.

You tap the message that applies. The message is sent as a text right away, which alerts the caller that you're not ignoring him — it's just that you can't talk right now. Nice touch.

You can also create and store your own message, like "Go away and leave me alone," or "Whatever I am doing is more important than talking to you." You could also be polite. To create your own canned message, tap Compose new message and type away. It's then stored on your phone for when you need it.

REMEMBER

The caller has to be able to receive text messages on the phone used to make the call. This feature doesn't work if your caller is calling from a landline or a cellphone that can't receive texts.

Keeping Track of Your Calls: The Recents

One of the nice features of cellular phones is that the phone keeps a record of the calls that you've made and received. Sure, you might have caller ID on your landline at home or work, but most landline phones don't keep track of whom you called. Cellphones, on the other hand, keep track of all the numbers you called. This information can be quite convenient, like when you want to return a call and you don't have that number handy. In addition, you can easily add a number to the contact list on your phone.

By tapping the Recent link on the phone screen, you get a list of all incoming and outgoing calls. (This hyperlink is located toward the top of the screen shown on the left side in Figure 3-2.) When you tap the Recent hyperlink, you see a call log like the one shown in Figure 3-6.

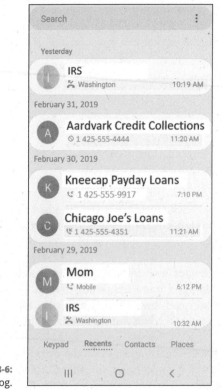

FIGURE 3-6:
A call log.

The tabs along the top include

>> **Outgoing call you made:** An orange arrow points to the number.

>> **Incoming call you received:** A green arrow points away from the number.

>> **Incoming call you missed:** A red phone silhouette with a broken arrow.

>> **Incoming call you ignored:** A blue slash sign is next to the phone number.

The log is a list of all the calls you made or were made to you. This is handy so that you can easily call someone again or call her back. By tapping any number in your call list, you see a screen like the one shown in Figure 3-7. From this screen, you can do several things:

>> Call the number by tapping the green call button.

>> Send a text to that number by tapping the orange envelope icon. (More on this in Chapter 4.)

>> Make a video call if you're set up to do that.

>> Tap the details icon to add the number to your contacts list. I cover contacts in more detail in Chapter 6.

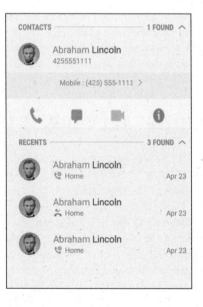

FIGURE 3-7:
Call Log detail.

Making an Emergency Call: The 411 on 911

Cellphones are wonderful tools for calling for help in an emergency. The Samsung Galaxy S10, like all phones in the United States and Canada, can make emergency calls to 911.

Just tap the Phone icon on the Home screen, tap 911, and then tap Send. You'll be routed to the 911 call center nearest to your location. This works wherever you're at within the United States. So, say you live in Chicago but have a car accident in Charlotte; just tap 911 to be connected to the 911 call center in Charlotte, not Chicago.

Even if your phone isn't registered on a network, you don't have a problem as long as you have a charge in the battery. You phone lets you know that the only number you can dial is a 911 call center, even if the Home screen is locked.

TIP

When you call 911 from a landline, the address you're calling from is usually displayed for the operator. When you're calling from a cellphone, though, the operator doesn't have that specific information. So, when you call 911, the operator might say, "911. *Where* is your emergency?" Don't let this question throw you; after all, you're probably focused on *what* is happening and not on *where*. Take a moment and come up with a good description of where you are — the street you're on, the nearest cross street (if you know it), any businesses or other landmarks nearby. An operator who knows where you are is in a better position to help you with your emergency. Your phone does have a GPS receiver in it that 911 centers can access. However, it's not always accurate; it may not be receiving location information at that moment, as is the case when you're indoors.

WHEN YOU ACCIDENTALLY DIAL 911

If you accidentally dial 911 from your phone, don't hang up. Just tell the operator that it was an accidental call. She might ask some questions to verify that you are indeed safe and not being forced to say that your call was an accident.

If you panic and hang up after accidentally dialing 911, you'll get a call from the nearest 911 call center. Always answer the call, even if you feel foolish. If you don't answer the call, the 911 call centers will assume that you're in trouble and can't respond. They'll track you down from the GPS in your phone to verify that you're safe. If you thought you'd feel foolish explaining your mistake to a 911 operator, imagine how foolish you'd feel explaining it to the police officer who tracks you down and is upset with you for wasting the department's time.

REMEMBER

When traveling outside the United States or Canada, 911 might not be the number you call in an emergency. Mexico uses 066, 060, or 080, but most tourist areas also accept 911. And most — but not all — of Europe uses 112. Knowing the local emergency number is as important as knowing enough of the language to say you need help.

Syncing a Bluetooth Headset

With a Bluetooth headset device, you can talk on your phone without having to hold the phone to your ear — and without any cords running from the phone to your earpiece. You've probably come across plenty of people talking on Bluetooth headsets. You might even have wondered whether they were a little crazy talking to themselves. Well, call yourself crazy now, because when you start using a Bluetooth headset, you might never want to go back.

Not surprisingly, Galaxy S10 phones can connect to Bluetooth devices. The first step to using a Bluetooth headset with your phone is to sync the two devices. Here's how:

1. **From the Home screen on your phone, slide up to get to the Apps screen.**

   This gets you to the list of all the applications on your phone.

2. **Flick or pan to the Settings icon and tap it.**

   The Settings icon is shown here. This screen holds most of the settings that you can adjust on your phone. If you prefer, you can also bring down the notification screen and tap the gear icon or tap the menu button on the Home screen. All these actions will get you to the same place.

   Tapping on the Settings icon brings up the screen shown in Figure 3-8.

3. **Tap the Connections icon.**

   All the options for connectivity on your phone appear.

4. **Tap the Bluetooth icon.**

   This will bring up one of the two screens shown in Figure 3-9. If Bluetooth is off, it will looks like the screen to the left. If it is on, it will look like the screen on the right.

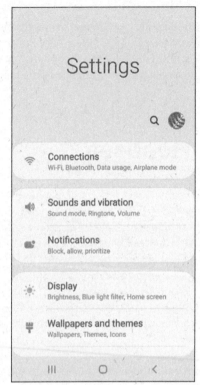

FIGURE 3-8:
The Settings
screen.

Bluetooth in "Off" Mode   Bluetooth in "On" Mode

< Connections Q		< Connections Q
Wi-Fi		**Wi-Fi**
Connect to Wi-Fi networks.		Connect to Wi-Fi networks.
Bluetooth		**Bluetooth**
Connect to nearby Bluetooth devices.		On

FIGURE 3-9:
The Bluetooth
Settings screens.

5. **Put the phone in to Pairing mode by turning on Bluetooth or by turning Bluetooth off and on again.**

This step enables your phone to be visible to other Bluetooth devices. This state will last for about 60 seconds — enough time for you to get your Bluetooth device into pairing mode so that both devices can negotiate the proper security settings and pair up every time they "see" each other from now on. For example, the phone in the right image in Figure 3-9 recognizes its old friend, the Plantronics Backbeat Pro. This device and the phone are shown in this image trying to re-establish a connection. The Backbeat Pro and this phone had a connection at one time. That connection was broken. Now they want to pair up again. This is automatic once you exchange the correct security code.

6. **Next, put your headset into sync mode.**

   Follow the instructions that came with your headset.

   After a moment, the phone "sees" the headset. When it does, you're prompted to enter the security code, and the software keyboard pops up.

7. **Enter the security code for your headset and then tap the Enter button.**

TIP

   The security code on most headsets is 0000, but check the instructions that came with your headset if that number doesn't work.

   Your phone might see other devices in the immediate area. If so, it asks you which device you want to pair with. Tap the name of your headset.

   Your headset is now synced to your phone. If you turn one on when the other is already on, they recognize each other and automatically pair up.

TIP

Some manufacturers make it easier to link via Bluetooth. For example, you may have received a pair of Samsung Galaxy Buds. With these ear buds, you simply open the case where you store the buds with your phone in scan mode. You're asked to connect, and it's all done. Don't be surprised when it's even easier than the steps listed in this section!

Options Other than Headsets

Headsets are not the only option anymore. Although many people walk around with the ubiquitous Bluetooth headset dangling from an ear, many other choices are out there. You can sync to all kinds of Bluetooth devices, including external keyboards, laptops, tablets, external speakers, and even your car.

There are also external sensors for measuring blood pressure, heart rate, and a lot of other physical information. Some of these are built into wearable devices, like a fitness bracelet. Manufacturers are now embedding computers into home appliances that can also connect to your smartphone through Bluetooth!

The good news is that regardless of the technology, you can connect all these devices to your phone simply by using the steps described in the preceding section. I talk more about these possibilities in later chapters.

Chapter **4**

Discovering the Joy of Text

S ure, cellphones are made for talking. But these days, many people use their cellphones even more for texting.

Even the most basic phones support texting these days, but your Galaxy S10 phone makes sending and receiving text messages more convenient, no matter whether you're an occasional or pathological texter. In this chapter, I fill you in on how to send a text message (with or without an attachment), how to receive a text message, and how to read your old text messages.

TIP

This chapter uses images from the Samsung Messaging application. It is possible that your phone may have as its default another texting application. If so, you can easily switch to the Messaging app. You can also use the default app, but the images will be somewhat different. Your choice.

Sending the First Text Message

Text messages (which are short messages, usually 160 characters or less, sent by cellphone) are particularly convenient when you can't talk at the moment (maybe you're in a meeting or class) or when you just have a small bit of information to share ("Running late — see you soon!").

Many cellphone users — particularly younger ones — prefer sending texts to making a phone call. They find texting a faster and more convenient way to communicate, and they often use texting shorthand to fit more content in a short message.

There are two scenarios for texting. The first is when you send someone a text for the first time. The second is when you have a text conversation with a person.

When you first get your phone and are ready to brag about your new Galaxy S10 and want to send a text to your best friend, here's how easy it is:

1. **On the Home screen, tap the Messages icon.**

   The Messages icon looks like an envelope. When you tap it, you will get a mostly blank Home screen for texting. This is shown in Figure 4-1.

   When you have some conversations going, it begins to fill up.

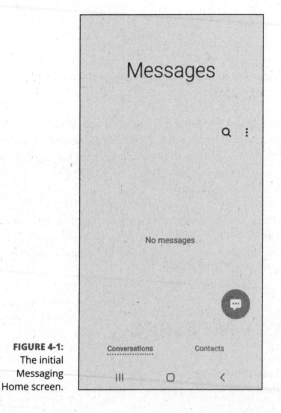

FIGURE 4-1:
The initial
Messaging
Home screen.

2. Tap the New Message icon (the cartoon talk bubble with the three dots).

Tapping the New Message icon brings up the screen shown in Figure 4-2.

FIGURE 4-2:
A blank texting
screen.

3. Tap to enter the recipient's ten-digit mobile telephone number.

A text box appears at the top of the screen with the familiar To field at the top. The keyboard appears at the bottom of the screen.

As shown in Figure 4-3, the top field is where you type the telephone number. The numerals are along the top of the keyboard.

REMEMBER

Be sure to include the area code, even if the person you're texting is local. There's no need to include a 1 before the number.

If this is your first text, you haven't had a chance to build up a history of texts. After you've been using your messaging application for a while, you will have entered contact information, and your phone will start trying to anticipate your intended recipient. You can take one of its suggestions or you can just keep on typing.

Partially typed number with guesses | Fully typed number

< NEW MESSAGE

4255555   ✕

(+)   425555

(A)   **Aaron C. Aardvark**
14255551617   Mobile

(B)   **Ben Franklin**
4255552222   Mobile

(G)   **George Washington**
4255559876   Mobile

(H)   **Herman Hermann**
4255554351   Mobile

Terry5th   Terry5   referring   >

1 2 3 4 5 6 7 8 9 0
q w e r t y u i o p
a s d f g h j k l
⇧ z x c v b n m ⌫
!@# 🎤 , English (US) . Next

< NEW MESSAGE

4255551216   ✕

(+)   4255551216

(+) [Enter message   😊] ➤

425555new6th   425555new6   425555dewy   >

1 2 3 4 5 6 7 8 9 0
q w e r t y u i o p
a s d f g h j k l
⇧ z x c v b n m ⌫
!@# 🎤 , English (US) . Next

FIGURE 4-3:
Type the
recipient's
number in the
upper text box.

4. **To type your text message, tap the text box that says Enter message. Figure 4-4 shows you where to enter your text.**

Your message will appear in the text box to the right of the paper clip icon.

In the Android Messaging app, your text message can be up to 160 characters, including spaces and punctuation. The application counts down the number of characters you have left.

REMEMBER

5. **Send the text by tapping the Send button to the right of your message.**

The Send button is grayed out before you start typing. After you type something, it turns full-on orange. Once you tap the button, the phone takes it from here. Within a few seconds, the message is sent to your friend's cellphone.

After you build your contact list (read about this in Chapter 6), you can tap a name from the contact list or start typing a name in the recipient text box. If there's only one number for that contact, your phone assumes that's the receiving phone you want to send a text to. If that contact has multiple numbers, it asks you which phone number you want to send your text to.

TIP

FIGURE 4-4:
Type your text.

REMEMBER

In most cases, the default for your texting app is for your phone to automatically correct what it thinks is a misspelled word. You can see it guess on the darker gray area under the text message. This capability is called *autocorrect*. You may find it very handy, or you may find it annoying. If you like it, you should still verify that it corrected the word in the right way. If you want evidence as to why this is a good idea, search "funny autocorrect examples" in your favorite search engine (although some can be very racy).

WARNING

You've probably heard a thousand times about how it's a very bad idea to text while you're driving. Here comes one-thousand-and-one. It's a *very bad idea* to text while you're driving — and illegal in many places. There are Dummies who read this book, who are actually very smart, and then there are DUMMIES who text and drive. I want you to be the former and not the latter.

Carrying on a Conversation via Texting

In the bad ol' pre-Galaxy S days, most cellular phones would keep a log of your texts. The phone kept the texts that you sent or received in sequential order, regardless of who sent or received them.

Texts stored sequentially are old-school. Your Galaxy S10 keeps track of the contact with whom you've been texting and stores each set of back-and-forth messages as a *conversation*.

In Figure 4-5, you can see that the first page for messaging holds *conversations*. After you start texting someone, those texts are stored in one conversation.

FIGURE 4-5:
A messaging
conversation.

As Figure 4-5 shows, each text message is presented in sequence, with the author of the text indicated by the direction of the text balloon.

Note the Enter message text box at the bottom of the screen. With this convenient feature, you can send whatever you type to the person with whom you're having a conversation.

In the bad old days, it was sometimes hard to keep straight the different texting conversations you were having. When you start a texting conversation with someone else, there is a second conversation.

Before too long, you'll have multiple conversations going on. Don't worry. They aren't the kind of conversations you need to keep going constantly. No one thinks twice if you don't text for a while. The image in Figure 4-6 shows how the text page from Figure 4-1 can look before too long.

CONVERSATIONS	CONTACTS

Bill Baden-Powell
Mike Q. is a foo...   6:19 PM

Bill Boyce
LOL. Chris thinks that..   3:16 PM

Quinlan Carbot
I am outside waiting..   7:52 AM

Mom
Eat your veggies   3:16 PM

Arlen E.
Can I have a new...   8:00 AM

Ellis Hamburg
Actually, the right ans..   3:16 PM

Indy Patricia Allen
Let's throw the ball!   3:16 PM

FIGURE 4-6:
The Text screen showing multiple conversations.

TIP

It is easy to change the font size of conversations. To make the fonts larger and easier to read, use the stretch motion. Use the pinch motion to make the fonts smaller so that you can see more of the conversation.

Sending an Attachment with a Text

What if you want to send something in addition to or instead of text? Say you want to send a picture, some music, or a Word document along with your text. Easy as pie, as long as the phone on the receiving end can recognize the attachment. Here is the recipe:

1. **From the Home screen, tap the Messages icon.**

2. **Either tap the New Message icon and enter the number of the intended recipient or pick up on an existing conversion.**

You'll see the Enter Message bubble from Figure 4-2. Enter the information you want like a normal text.

3. **To add an attachment, tap the plus sign to the left of where you enter text.**

    The plus sign brings up the screen you see in Figure 4-7, which asks what kind of file you want to attach. Your choices include pictures, videos, audio files, and some others I describe in Chapters 9, 12, 13, and 14 when you have some good files to share. For now, it's just good that you know you have options.

Photos stored on your phone

Photos you take right now

Drawings   Your location

Files from any of the apps listed below

4. **Tap your choice of file type, and your phone presents you with the options that fall into that category.**

    Get ready to be amazed. Underneath the text box, you have five choices. These include the Gallery for photos, a shot you can take now with the camera, a doodle, a map with your location, or other categories. Figure 4-7 shows the Other category. This is for any file you want to attach that is already on your phone. It can be your electronic business card. It could be a video.

    The Quick response opens up canned responses, such as "What's up?" or "Where's the meeting?" How cool is that?!

5. Continue typing your text message, if needed.

6. When you're done with the text portion of the message, tap the Send button (the one that looks like a line drawing of a paper airplane), and off it all goes.

TECHNICAL STUFF

A simple text message is an SMS (short message service) message. When you add an attachment, you're sending an MMS (multimedia messaging service) message. Back in the day, MMS messages cost more to send and receive than SMS messages did. These days, that isn't the case in the United States.

Receiving Text Messages

Receiving a text is even easier than sending one.

When you're having a text conversation and you get a new text from the person you're texting with, your phone beeps and/or vibrates. Also, the notification area of the screen (the very top) shows a very small version of the Messages icon.

You can either pull down the notification area from the very top of the screen or start the messaging application. Your choice.

If an attachment comes along, it's included in the conversation screen.

To access the text, you need to unlock the screen. The Messages icon (an envelope) also displays the number of new texts that you have. Tap that icon to open the conversations.

Managing Your Text History

The Messaging Conversations screen stores and organizes all your texts until you delete them. You should clean up this screen every now and then.

The simplest option for managing your messages is to tap the Menu icon and then tap Delete. You can then select and unselect all the conversations that you want deleted. Tap the icon that looks like a garbage can at the bottom of the screen, and they disappear.

Another deletion option is to open the conversation. You can delete each text by pressing and holding on the balloon. After a moment, a menu appears from which you can delete that message. This method is a lot slower if you have lots of texts, though.

I recommend that you be vicious in deleting the older texts and conversations. Trust me; deleting all your old messages can be cathartic!

Chapter **5**

Sending and Receiving Email

I f you've had email on your phone for a while, you know how convenient it is. If your Galaxy S10 phone is your first cellphone with the capability to send and receive email, prepare to be hooked.

I start this chapter by showing you how to set up your email, regardless of whether your email program is supported. Then I show you how to read and manage your email. Finally, I tell you how to write and send email in the last section in this chapter.

Setting Up Your Email

These days, many people have multiple personal email address for many reasons. Your phone's Email app can manage up to ten email accounts. With a Galaxy S10 phone, you may need to create a separate email account on Google's Gmail just for your phone. If you do not get a Gmail account, you'll miss out on so many exciting capabilities. I highly recommend setting up a new Gmail account if you don't have one already (see the upcoming section "Setting up a new Gmail account").

The Email app on your phone routinely "polls" all the email systems for which you identify an email account and password. It then presents you with copies of your email.

TIP

Your phone mainly interacts with your inbox on your email account. It isn't really set up to work like the full-featured email application on your computer, though. For example, many email packages integrate with a sophisticated word processor, have sophisticated filing systems for your saved messages, and offer lots of fonts. As long as you don't mind working without these capabilities, you might never need to get on your computer to access your email again, and you could store email in folders on your phone.

Setup is easy, and having access to all your email makes you so productive that I advise you to consider adding all your email accounts to your phone.

Getting ready

In general, connecting to a personal email account simply involves entering the name of your email account(s) and its password(s) in your phone. Have these handy when you're ready to set up your phone.

As mentioned, you can have up to ten email accounts on your phone; however, you do need to pick one account as your favorite. You can send an email using any of the accounts, but your phone wants to know the email account that you want it to use as a default.

Next, you may want to have access to your work account. This is relatively common these days, but some companies see this as a security problem. You should consult with your IT department for some extra information. Technologically, it's not hard to make this kind of thing happen as long as your business email is reasonably modern.

Finally, if you don't already have a Gmail account, I strongly encourage you to get one. Read the nearby sidebar, "The advantages of getting a Gmail account" to find out why.

Setting up your existing Gmail account

If you already have a Gmail account, setting it up on your phone is easy as can be. Follow these steps from the Apps menu:

1. **Find the Gmail icon in the Apps list.**

   Here is a confusing part. The icon on the left in Figure 5-1 is the Gmail app. The icon on the right is for the general email app. The general email app is for your combined email accounts. The general email account is the app that you will use to access any and all of your email accounts.

FIGURE 5-1:
The Email and
Gmail icons.

2. **Tap the Gmail icon.**

   Because your phone does not know if you have a Gmail account yet, it offers you the option of entering your Gmail account or whether you want to create a new account. This page is shown in Figure 5-2.

THE ADVANTAGES OF GETTING A GMAIL ACCOUNT

You might already have work and personal email accounts. You might even have an old email account that you check only once in a while because some friends, for whatever reason, haven't updated their profile for you and continue to use an old address.

The thought of getting yet another email address, even one that's free, might (understandably) be unappealing. After all, it's another address and password to remember. However, some important functions on your phone require a Gmail account:

- The ability to buy applications from the Google Play Store. (This is big!) I go over the Play Store in Chapter 8.

- The ability to use the Google Drive for storage. (This is pretty important and almost huge!)

- Free access to the photo site Google Photos (although other sites have many of the same features).

- Automatic backup of your contacts and calendar. That's explained in more detail in Chapters 6 and 13.

To make a long story short, it's worth the trouble to get a Gmail account, even if you already have a personal email account.

FIGURE 5-2:
Add your
account page.

3. **Enter your Gmail account email address and tap Next.**

   Be sure to include the @gmail.com suffix.

4. **Enter your existing Gmail password and tap Next.**

   Go ahead and type your password. When you're ready, tap Next on the keyboard.

You may get a pop-up reconfirming that you agree with the terms of use and all that legal stuff. Tap OK. You'll see lots of flashing lights and whirling circles while your phone and your Gmail account get to know each other.

If everything is correct, your phone and your account get acquainted and become best friends. After a few minutes, they are ready to serve your needs. There are even a few screens that tell you all the wonderful things that your Gmail account will do for you. Believe every word!

If you have a problem, you probably mistyped something. Try retyping your information. From this point on, any email you get in your Gmail account will also appear on your phone!

Setting up a new Gmail account

If you need to set up a new Gmail account, you have a few more steps to follow. Before you get into the steps, think up a good user ID and password.

TIP

Gmail has been around for a while. That means all the good, simple email addresses are taken. Unless you plan to start using this email account as your main email, which you could do if you wanted, you're probably best off if you pick some unusual combination of letters and numbers that you can remember for now to get through this process.

When you have all of this ready, follow Steps 1 and 2 in the previous section, but tap the Create Account link when you get to the screen shown in Figure 5-2. From there, follow these steps:

1. **Enter your first and last names on the screen.**

   Google asks for your name in the screen shown in Figure 5-3. This is how Google personalizes any communications it has with you.

   TIP

   You may be tempted to use a fake name or some other clever two-word combination in place of a name. Don't do it. You will still be getting email to Rita Book or Warren Peace long after the humor has worn off.

FIGURE 5-3:
The Create your
Google Account
screen.

Google · Sign in

Create your Google Account

Name
Nikola | Tesla

Choose your username
Edisonisajerk-ACRules@gmail.com
I prefer to use my current email address

Create a password
****

Password strength:
Use at least 8 characters. Don't use a password from another site, or something too obvious like your pet's name. Why?

Confirm your password
****

Birthday
July | 10 | 1856

Gender
Male

Mobile phone
United States +1
+1 201 555-1100

Your current email address
Nikola@wardenclyfetower.com

Location
United States

Continue

Learn more about why we ask for this information.

2. **Enter the username you want to use with Gmail.**

On the screen shown in Figure 5-3, enter the username you want. Hopefully you get this name approved on the first shot.

If your first choice isn't available, try again. There is no easy way to check before you go through these steps. Eventually, you hit on an unused ID, or you will use one of the suggestions in blue font. When you're successful, it will congratulate you.

3. **Pick a good password of at least eight characters.**

Be sure to pick one that is unique and that you can remember.

4. **Enter the other information and an alternate email address and tap Continue.**

If you forget your password, Google wants to verify that you're really you and not someone pretending to be you. Google does this check by sending a confirmation email to another account or sending a text to your phone. You can do this now or tap Skip to do it later.

After you tap Done, light flashes, and you see the screen working away. This process usually takes less than two minutes. While you wait, you'll see all kinds of messages that it's getting ready to sync things. Don't worry. I explain these messages in good time. For now, you can add any other email accounts you want by following the steps in the next section.

Working with non-Gmail email accounts

Your phone is set up to work with up to ten email accounts. If you have more than ten accounts, I'm thinking that you might have too much going on in your life. No phone, not even the Galaxy S10, can help you there!

I now cover the steps to adding your email accounts. Once you tell your phone all your email accounts, the Email screen will let you see the inbox of each account or combine all your email in a single inbox. You can choose which option works best for you.

Adding your first email account

To get started, have your email addresses and passwords ready. When you have them, go to your phone's Home screen. Look for the Mail icon; it is an envelope in silhouette (refer to Figure 5-1). This is probably on your Home screen as one of the four primary shortcuts just above the Device Function keys or in your application list.

1. **Tap the Mail icon from the Home screen.**

   This brings up a screen like the one shown in Figure 5-4. Choose one of the options to get started. In every case, it starts with entering your email address.

WARNING

   Your email address should include the full shebang, including the @ sign and everything that follows it. Make sure to enter your password correctly, being careful with capitalization if your email server is case-sensitive (most are). If in doubt, select the option that lets you see your password.

FIGURE 5-4:
The setup
screen for the
Email app.

2. **Tap the box to enter your password.**

   Don't be surprised if your S10 brings you to a special screen specifically for your email provider for you to enter your password. Figure 5-5 shows the sign-in screen for a generic email account. Figure 5-6 shows the screen for a Microsoft Exchange account. One of these will work.

3. **Carefully enter your password in the appropriate field and tap Next.**

   You're asked for permissions. Just go with the default settings for now. This brings up the screen shown in Figure 5-7.

4. **Select your desired Sync Settings and then tap Next.**

   You can select how often you want your phone and the email service to synchronize. A lot of thought and consideration has been put into the default settings. If you just want to get started, tap Next.

   If you want to fine-tune things later, it is not hard to go back and adjust these settings. These settings are intended to be gentle on your data usage.

FIGURE 5-7:
The Sync
Settings screen.

If you want images in email to download immediately, store older email messages on your phone, check to see whether you have new email all the time, you can change these settings on this page for this email account. If you know what you want that is different from the default settings, make the changes and then tap Next.

5. **Enter a name for the new email account.**

The next screen is shown in Figure 5-8. This gives you the option to call your email account something other than its address. You can call it what you like, but I recommend choosing something shorter, like Joe's MSN or My Hotmail. (Do as I say, not as I do.)

6. **Tap Done.**

Using Figure 5-9 as an example, you can see that my account is now registered on my phone. It worked!

FIGURE 5-8:
Naming your
email account.

Options icon

FIGURE 5-9:
The Email Home
screen.

Adding additional email accounts

Once you have entered your first email account, there are a few different steps to add additional accounts.

1. **Tap the Options icon at the top-left part of the screen.**

The three horizontal lines bring up the slide-in screen shown in Figure 5-10. This allows you to see other email folders. It also lets you access the setting icon.

galaxysfordummies@gmai...

galaxysfordum
mies@gmail
.com

Somebody@something.com

All accounts

Inbox

Unread

VIP VIPs

Starred

Sent

FIGURE 5-10:
The Options
slide-in screen.

2. **Tap the Settings icon.**

Tapping Settings brings up the screen shown in Figure 5-11.

3. **Tap Add Account next to the green plus sign.**

This brings you back to the email setup screen (refer to Figure 5-5).

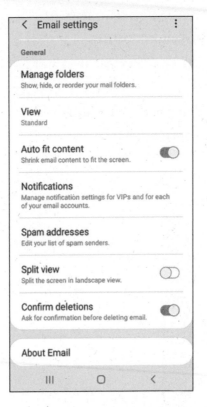

FIGURE 5-11:
The Email
Settings screen.

At this point you can add up to nine more accounts, and remember, you will be asked which email account you want to be your primary account. It is entirely up to you. You can send and receive email from all your accounts by selecting it, but only one can be the primary account used if you send an email from another application, such as the Contacts app.

Setting up a corporate email account

In addition to personal email accounts, you can add your work email account to your phone — if it's based upon a Microsoft Exchange server, that is, and if it's okay with your company's IT department.

Before you get started, you need some information from the IT department of your company:

>> The domain name of the office email server.

>> Your work email password.

>> The name of your exchange server.

If the folks in IT are okay with you using your phone to access its email service, your IT department will have no trouble supplying you with this information.

WARNING

Before you set up your work email on your phone, make sure that you have permission. If you do this without the green light from your company, and you end up violating your company's rules, you could be in hot water. Increasing your productivity won't be much help if you're standing out in the parking lot holding all the contents of your office in a cardboard box.

Assuming that your company wants you to be more productive with no extra cost to the company, the process for adding your work email starts at your email Home screen shown in Figure 5-5.

1. **Enter your email address and password.**

The Corporate screen is shown in Figure 5-12.

← Exchange ActiveSync

Configure Exchange account in a few steps.

bigwig@powermadcorp.com

••••••••••

☐ Show password

☐ Set this account as the default for sending emails.

MANUAL SETUP   NEXT >

FIGURE 5-12:
The Corporate set up email screen.

2. **Tap Manual Setup.**

This brings up the screen shown in Figure 5-13.

The chances are that you haven't got the foggiest notion what any of this means or what you are to do now.

← Exchange server settings

Email address
bigwig@powermadcorp.com

Domain\username
\bigwig

Password
•••••••••

☐ Show password

Exchange server
Powermadcorp.com

☑ Use secure connection (SSL)

☐ Use client certificate

CLIENT CERTIFICATE

NEXT >

FIGURE 5-13:
The Manual
Setup screen for
adding corporate
email accounts.

3. **Verify that your IT department is good with you having email on your own device and have them give you the necessary settings.**

Seriously. It is increasingly common that a firm will give you access on your phone. At the same time, they do not generally circulate documents with how to make this happen. This would be a big security problem if anyone could get access. Save yourself the time and get help from IT.

Reading Email on Your Phone

In Figure 5-9, you can see how the email screen looks for what I have called My Personal Email. You can also set it up so that this screen is set up so that it combines all your email into one inbox. At any given time, you might want to look at the accounts individually or all together.

To look at all your email in one large inbox, tap the downward pointing arrow next to the word Inbox and select Combined Inbox. This lists all your email in chronological order. To open any email message, just tap it.

If, on the other hand, you want to see just email from one account, tap the box at the top that says Combined Inbox. When you tap this icon, your phone will display all the individual email accounts. Tap on the account you want to focus on at the moment, and your phone will bring up your email in chronological order for just that email address.

Writing and Sending Email

 After you set up the receiving part of email, the other important side is composing and sending email. At any time when you're in an email screen, simply tap the Menu button to get a pop-up screen. From the pop-up menu, tap the Compose icon to open the email composition screen.

Here's the logic that determines which email account will send this email:

» If you're in the inbox of an email account and you tap the Compose icon after tapping Menu, your phone sends the email to the intended recipient(s) through that account.

» If you're in the combined inbox or some other part of the email app, your phone assumes that you want to send the email from the default email account that you selected when you registered your second (or additional) email account.

When you tap the Compose icon in the Menu pop-up menu, it tells you which account it will use. The Email composition screen shown in Figure 5-14 says this email will be coming from this account: galaxysfordummies@gmail.com.

As shown in this screen, the top has a stalwart To field, where you type the recipient's address. You can also call up your contacts, a group, or your most recent email addresses. (Read all about contacts in Chapter 6.) Tap the address or contact you want, and it populates the To field.

Below that, in the Subject field, is where you enter the email's topic. And below that is the body of the message, with the default signature, *Sent from my Samsung Galaxy S10,* although your cellular carrier might have customized this signature.

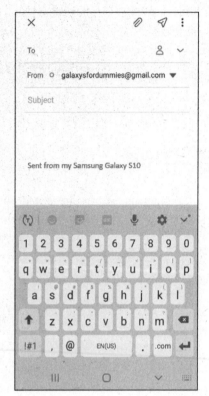

FIGURE 5-14:
The Email
composition
screen.

At the top of the screen are three links:

>> **Attach:** Tap this hyperlink to attach a file of any variety to your email.

>> **Send:** Tap this icon that looks like a paper airplane to send the email to the intended recipient(s).

>> **More (three vertical dots):** Tap this option, and you get the pop-up shown in Figure 5-15. This may give you some of the following options:

- **Save in Drafts:** This allows you to complete the email later without losing your work.

- **Send email to myself:** This is an alternative to saving the email in your Sent mail folder.

- **Priority:** This option signifies that this is more important that the average email to your recipients.

- **Security options:** You have some fancy, 007 options here. You can sign the document or encrypt it.

- **Turn on Rich text:** To save data usage, email is sent in a default font. If you want to burn at little more data, you can get creative and add more elaborate fonts.

FIGURE 5-15:
Composition
email options.

Save in Drafts
Send email to myself
Priority
Security options
Turn on Rich text

If you change your mind about sending an email message, you can just tap the Back key. If you're partially done with the message, you're asked whether you want to save it in your Drafts folder.

The Drafts folder works like the Drafts folder in your computer's email program. When you want to continue working on a saved email, you open the Drafts folder, tap on it, and continue working.

Replying To and Forwarding Email

Replying to or forwarding the email that you get is a common activity. You can do this from your Email app. Figure 5-16 shows a typical open email message.

You can reply by tapping the icon with the return arrow at the bottom of the screen. If other people were copied on the email, you could tap the double return arrow to Reply all.

When you tap either of these options, the Reply screen comes back with the To line populated by the sender's email address (or addresses) and a blank space where you can leave your comments. (In the case of Figure 5-16, you could ask that your dad not send you any more jokes like these.)

Dad Jokes

February 30, 2019 11:27AM

Dad   DETAILS

                                    SHOW IMAGES

I bought a bad Thesaurus. It was so bad, it was bad.

Did you hear about the guy who invented LifeSavers®? He made a mint!

A sandwich walks into a bar and orders a beer. The bartender says, "Sorry, we don't serve food here."

Did you hear the rumor going around about peanut butter? Never mind. I shouldn't spread it.

People frequently ask what I want to be doing in a few years. I don't know. I don't have 2020 vision.

There are three kinds of people in this world: Those that are good at math and those that are not.

I decided to sell my vacuum cleaner. It was just gathering dust.

What did the hungry clock do? It went back four seconds.

Reply   Reply all   Forward   Delete   Thread

FIGURE 5-16:
An opened
email.

To forward the email, tap the arrow pointing to the right above the word Forward and enter the addressee just as you do when sending a new email.

Chapter **6**

Managing Your Contacts

You're probably familiar with using contact databases. Many cellphones automatically create one, or at least prompt you to create one. You also probably have a file of contacts on your work computer, made up of work email addresses and telephone numbers. And if you have a personal email account, you probably have a contact database of email accounts of friends and family members. If you're kickin' it old school, you might even keep a paper address book with names, addresses, and telephone numbers.

The problem with having all these contact databases is that it's rarely ever as neat and tidy as I've just outlined. A friend might email you at work, so you have her in both your contact databases. Then her email address might change, and you update that information in your personal address book but not in your work one. Before long, you have duplicate and out-of-date contacts, and it's hard to tell which is correct. How you include Facebook or LinkedIn messaging in your contact profile is unclear.

In addition to problems keeping all your contact databases current, it can be a hassle to migrate the database from your old phone. Some cellular carriers or firms have offered a service that converts your existing files to your new phone, but it's rarely a truly satisfying experience. You end up spending a lot of time correcting the assumptions it makes.

You now face that dilemma again with your Galaxy S10: deciding how to manage your contacts. This chapter gives you the advantages of each approach so that you can decide which one will work best for you. That way, you won't have the frustration of wishing you had done it another way before you put 500 of your best friends in the wrong filing system.

Using the Galaxy S10 Contacts App

Your phone wants you to be able to communicate with all the people you would ever want to in any way you know how to talk to them. This is a tall order, and your Galaxy S10 makes it as easy as possible. In fact, I wouldn't be surprised if the technology implemented in the Contacts app becomes one of your favorite capabilities of the phone. After all, your phone is there to simplify communication with friends, family, and coworkers, and the Contacts app on your phone makes it as easy as technology allows.

At the same time, this information is only as good as your contact database discipline. The focus of this section is to help you help your phone help you.

Learning the Contacts App on your phone

The fact of the matter is, if you introduced your phone to your email accounts in Chapter 5, the Contacts list on your phone has all the contacts from each of your contact lists.

 Take a look at it and see. From your Home screen, tap the Contacts icon.

If you haven't created a Gmail account, synced your personal email, or created a contact when you sent a text or made a call, your Contacts list will be empty. Otherwise, you see a bunch of your contacts now residing on your phone, sorted alphabetically (as shown in Figure 6-1).

Along with the Contacts application that manages the data, this database does more than just store names, phone numbers, and email addresses. However, you can have the contact include any or all of the following information:

>> All telephone numbers, including

- Mobile

- Home

- Work

- Work fax

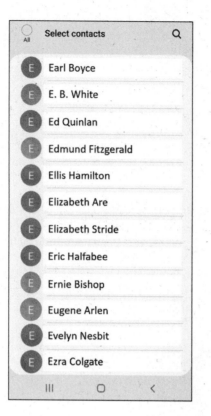

FIGURE 6-1:
The Contacts list.

- • Pager
- • Other
- » Email addresses
  - • Home
  - • Work
  - • Mobile
- » Instant Messaging addresses
- » Company/organization
- » Job title
- » Nickname
- » Mailing address for
  - • Home
  - • Work
  - • Another location

Select contacts   🔍
All

Earl Boyce

E. B. White

Ed Quinlan

Edmund Fitzgerald

Ellis Hamilton

Elizabeth Are

Elizabeth Stride

Eric Halfabee

Ernie Bishop

Eugene Arlen

Evelyn Nesbit

Ezra Colgate

||| ◯   ‹

>> Any notes about this person

- Web address

- Birthday (or other significant event)

- A phonetic spelling of the name

As if all this weren't enough, you can assign a specific ringtone to play when a particular person contacts you. I cover the steps to assign a music file to an individual caller in Chapter 12.

Finally, you can assign a picture for the contact. It can be one out of your Gallery; you can take a new picture; or (as I discuss in Chapter 8) you can connect to a social network like Facebook and use that person's profile picture.

Fortunately, the only essential information is a name. Every other field is optional and is only displayed if the field contains information to be displayed. Figure 6-2 shows a lightly populated contact.

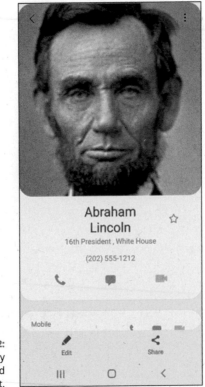

FIGURE 6-2:
A lightly
populated
contact.

Deciding where to store your contacts

Before we get too far, it is important for you to decide the default option where you want to store your contacts. Deciding this now with the information this section provides you will make your life much easier as you go forward. It is possible to combine contact databases, but even the best tools are imperfect.

The first time you try to save a new contact, the Contacts App will offer you a pop-up screen, as shown in Figure 6-3. This lists the options you have and will take your first entry as the option you want as a default.

Save contact to

- ○ Samsung account
  Somebody@something.com

- ○ Phone

- ○ Google
  Galaxysfordummies@gmail.com

- ○ SIM card

- ○ Microsoft Exchange ActiveSync
  Somebody@something.com

Select | Set as default

FIGURE 6-3: Choosing a default for creating new contacts.

Whenever you save a new entry, you can manually switch to another of these databases. Save yourself some time and aggravation and decide now what you want to do. Here are your options on where to save new contacts:

>> Within the memory of your phone.

>> On the SIM card inserted in your phone.

>> Within your Gmail account.

>> As a contact in one of your other accounts.

Each of these four options has advantages and disadvantages. If you simply want my advice, I suggest using your Gmail account to store new contacts. If this satisfies you, skip to the next section on linking contacts from other sources. Read on if you need some context.

Here is the deal: If everything is working properly, all options work equally well. However, if you switch phones regularly, ever lose you phone, need to make significant updates to your contacts, or are frequently out of wireless coverage, such as on an airplane, you should consider the options.

The first option mentioned involves storing your contacts within your phone. This is a great option, as long as you have your phone. However, there will come a day when Samsung (or HTC, or LG, and so on) has something faster and better, and you will want to upgrade. At that point, perhaps next year or in ten years, you will need to move your contacts to another location if you want to keep them. Plus, if you lose your phone, I sure hope that you have recently used one of the backup options I explore in Chapter 17.

The second option is to store your new contacts on your SIM card. The SIM card is familiar technology if your previous phone worked with AT&T or T-Mobile. Figure 6-4 shows a profile of a typical SIM card, next to a dime for scale, although yours probably has the logo of your cellular carrier nicely printed on the card. To the right of the SIM card is the newer micro SIM card. This is the same idea, but in a smaller package.

FIGURE 6-4:
A SIM card and a micro SIM card.

TECHNICAL STUFF

If your cellular carrier is Verizon, Sprint, or US Cellular, you may be confused. Your Galaxy S10 has a SIM card. What's the story? These carriers use CDMA technology for voice and for some data features. Up to 3G, the phones using CDMA technology and data services didn't use a SIM card. Today, *all* carriers in the United States are implementing a super high-speed data technology called LTE, also called 4G. Because your phone is capable of LTE, you now have a SIM card.

The cool aspect of using your SIM card is that you can pluck it out of your existing phone and pop it in another phone and all your contacts come with you. It works this easily if you stay with an Android smartphone of recent vintage. It almost works this easily if you, say, switch back to a feature phone (as in the kind of phone that merely makes calls and texts and costs $1). Another advantage is that your SIM card does not rely on having a wireless connection to update changes.

The next option is to store new contacts on your Gmail account. What this means is that your new contacts are automatically copied from your phone to the Gmail account of Google servers. This keeps the records on your phone, but Google maintains a copy of this record in your Gmail account. You can make changes to a contact on your phone or on your PC.

The two reasons I recommend using your Gmail account are:

>> You can maintain these records with your full-sized keyboard rather than the smaller keyboard on your phone.

>> It is easy to get back all these contacts on a new Android phone simply by telling the new phone your Gmail account. Because you will probably enter your Gmail account right away when you get a new phone, your contacts reappear quicker than the fourth option.

The fourth option is to store the contacts in one of your existing email accounts. This may be the best option if you already consider your email, either your personal or work account, to be the primary location where you store contacts. If you already have good database discipline with one of your email accounts, by all means, use this email account as the default place to store new contacts.

If this particular account you currently use for keeping your contacts is not set up yet on your phone, you can tap the Add New Account link shown in Figure 6-3 to go through the process described in Chapter 5 to set up a new email account.

Linking Contacts on your phone

The Contacts list is smart. Allow me to explain some of the things that are going on.

Say your best friend is Bill McCarty, affectionately known as "the Kid." You sent Bill a text earlier to let him know about your new phone. You followed the instructions on how to send a text in Chapter 4 and entered his telephone number. You took it to the next step and tapped Add Contact. When you were prompted to add his name, you did. Now your phone has a contact, "Bill McCarty."

Then you linked your email. Of course your buddy Bill is in your email Contacts list. So while you were reading this chapter, several things happened. First, these two contacts automatically synced. Your phone thinks about it and figures this must be the same person. It automatically combines all the information in one entry on your phone!

Then your phone automatically updates your Gmail account. On the left side of Figure 6-5, you see Bill's mobile number. This contact is synced with your Gmail account. You didn't have to do anything to make this happen.

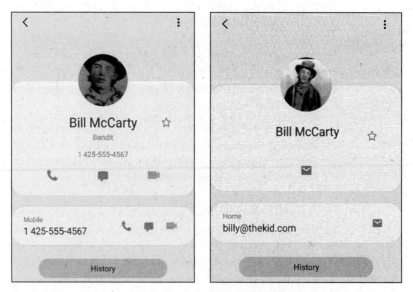

FIGURE 6-5:
Two contacts for
the same person.

Your phone noticed that Bill's work number was in your email contact information, but the mobile phone number you used to text him was not. No problem! Now the contact on your phone includes both the information you had in your email contact as well as his cellular phone.

Now, as slick as this system is, it isn't perfect. In this scenario, both contacts have the same first and last name. However, if the same person also goes by a different name, you have to link these contacts. For example, if you created a contact for Bill McCarty, but your email refers to him as William H. McCarty, your phone will assume that these are two different people. This is shown in Figure 6-6.

Options

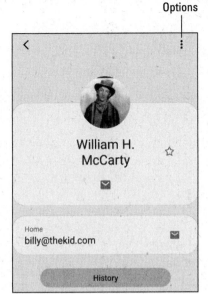

FIGURE 6-6:
The Linking Page
for Bill McCarty.

No problem, though. Do you see the three vertical dots in Figure 6-6? Here are the steps to link the two contacts for the same person:

1. **From a contact, tap on the three vertical dots.**

   This brings up the pop-up shown in Figure 6-7.

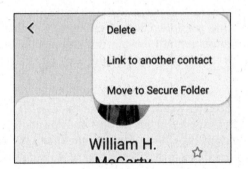

FIGURE 6-7:
The pop-up to
with the linking
suggestions.

2. **Tap the Link Another Contact link.**

   Your phone will try to help you with some suggestions. If it gets it all wrong, you can just find the other contact by searching alphabetically, as shown in Figure 6-8.

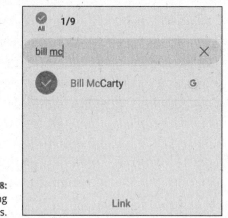

FIGURE 6-8:
The linking
suggestions.

3. **Tap the contact you want joined.**

   In this case, the second guess, Bill McCarty, is the one you want. Tap the face (or circle) to the left of his name and then the two contacts are linked.

TIP

4. **Now tap the link that says Link in the bottom center of the screen.**

   This combined link will now have all the information on this one person.

Creating Contacts within Your Database

Your phone is out there trying to make itself the ultimate contact database with as little effort on your part as possible. The interesting thing is that the salesperson in the cellular store probably didn't explain this to you in detail. It's a subtle-but-important capability that's hard to communicate on the sales floor. Here's what happens.

Whenever you make or receive a call, send or receive an email, or send or receive a text, your phone looks up the telephone number or email address from which the message originated to check whether it has seen that address before. If it has, it has all the other information on that person ready. If it doesn't recognize the originating telephone number or email, it asks whether you want to make it a new contact or update an existing one. What could be easier?

Adding contacts as you dial

When you get a call, a text, or an email from someone who isn't in your contacts, you're given the option to create a profile for that person. The same is true when you initiate contact with someone who isn't in your Contacts list. Chapter 3 shows you the empty and full dialing screens. The image on the left in Figure 6-9 shows the phone trying its best to anticipate the person you are in the process of calling, and, if it is not saved already, the image on the right shows how it offers you the option to add this number to your contacts.

FIGURE 6-9: The dialing screens in process and when there is a new number.

You're immediately given the option to create a contact or update an existing contact. Your phone doesn't know whether this is a new number for an existing contact or a totally new person. Rather than make an assumption (as lesser phones on the market would do), your phone asks you whether you need to create a new profile or add this contact information to an existing profile.

Keep in mind that if you are calling an existing contact and your phone guesses the right person, you can save yourself time and tap the phone to dial.

TIP

Say that you want to enter this number as a new contact. You follow these steps:

1. **Tap the Create Contact link.**

   A new contact page appears. An example is shown in Figure 6-10.

   The number is already populated. You just need to fill in the correct name plus any other information that you want associated with this person.

2. **When you're done typing in the information for this contact, tap Save at the top of the contact.**

   Figure 6-10 shows the Save button at the top of the screen.

FIGURE 6-10: A partially populated contact.

Adding contacts manually

Adding contacts manually involves taking an existing contact database and adding its entries to your phone, one profile at a time. (This option, a last resort, was the only option for phones back in the day.)

1. **Tap the Contacts icon.**

   Doing so brings up the list of existing contacts shown in Figure 6-1.

2. **Tap the Add Contacts icon (the + [plus] sign next to a silhouette).**

   This icon is shown in Figure 6-11. Tapping it will bring up a blank contact page with nothing populated.

FIGURE 6-11:
The Add
Contacts icon.

3. **Fill in the information you want to include.**

4. **When you're done entering data, tap Save at the top of the screen.**

   The profile is now saved. Repeat the process for as many profiles as you want to create.

How Contacts Make Life Easy

Phew. Heavy lifting over. After you populate the profiles of dozens or hundreds of contacts, you're rewarded with a great deal of convenience.

To contact someone from the contacts directory, start by tapping the contact icon. Your contacts list appears (refer to Figure 6-1). Scroll down or search for the contract you want. When you tap that contact name, you're given some choices, as shown in Figure 6-12.

FIGURE 6-12:
The Contacts
Database when
you tap a profile.

I've tapped on the contact for my friend, Ludwig, and I have choices:

>> Tap the green telephone next to the number to dial that number.

>> Tap the blue message icon to send a text.

>> Tap the green video call icon to have a video chat.

>> Tap the gray envelope icon to send an email.

About the only thing that tapping on a data field won't do is print an envelope for you if you tap the mailing address! At the bottom of the contact is a button that says History. This is a running log of all your communications with that contact regardless of the media you used. Figure 6–13 shows an example.

It is all there.

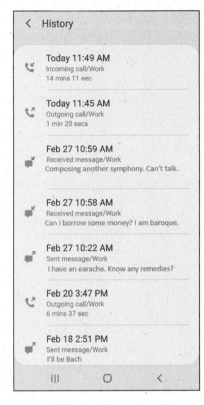

FIGURE 6-13:
Your history with
that person.

Playing Favorites

Over the course of time, you'll probably find yourself calling some people more than others. It would be nice to not have to scroll through your entire contacts database to find those certain people. Contacts allow you to place some of your contacts into a Favorites list for easy access.

From within the Contacts app, open the profile and notice the star next to that person's name (refer to Figure 6-12). To the right of the contact name is a star. If that star is gold, that contact is a Favorite. If not, then not.

To make a contact into a star, tap the blank outline of the star. To demote a contact from stardom without deleting, tap the gold star.

You won't immediately see a difference in your contacts other than the appearance of the gold star. When you open your phone, however, this contact now appears under your Favorites tab. The Favorites tab is like a mini-contact database. It looks similar in structure to your regular contact database, but it includes only your favorites.

3

Living on the Internet

IN THIS PART . . .

Surf the web from your phone.

Get to know Google's Play Store and add exciting new apps to your phone.

Chapter **7**

You've Got the Whole (Web) World in Your Hands

I f you're like most people, one of the reasons you got a smartphone is because you want Internet access on the go. You don't want to have to wait until you get back to your laptop or desktop to find the information you need online. You want to be able to access the Internet even when you're away from a Wi-Fi hotspot — and that's exactly what you can do with your Galaxy S10 phone. In this chapter, I show you how.

The browser that comes standard with your Galaxy S10 works almost identically to the browser that's currently on your PC. You see many familiar toolbars, including the Favorites bar and search engine. And the mobile version of the browser includes tabs that allow you to open multiple Internet sessions simultaneously.

This chapter goes into much more detail on using the Internet browser on your Galaxy S10, as well as the websites you can access from your phone, and discusses some of the trade-offs you can make when viewing a web page.

Starting the Browser

You have three options for getting access to information from the Internet via your Galaxy S10 phone. Which one you use is a personal choice. The choices are

>> **Use the regular web page:** This option involves accessing a web page via its regular address (URL) and having the page come up on your screen. The resulting text may be small.

>> **Use the mobile web page:** Almost all websites these days offer a mobile version of their regular web page. This is an abbreviated version of the full website that can be more easily read on a mobile device.

>> **Find out whether a mobile app is associated with the web page:** Many websites have found that it is most expedient to write a mobile application to access the information on its website. The app reformats the web page to fit better on a mobile screen — a convenient option if you plan to access this website regularly. I cover the trade-offs about this option later in the section "Deciding Between Mobile Browsing and Mobile Apps" and explore how to find and install such apps in Chapter 8.

With this background, head to the Internet. On your Galaxy S10 phone, you may have a few choices on how to get there. Figure 7-1 shows three possible icons that can get you there. Tap any of these, and you can start surfing.

FIGURE 7-1:
Possible paths to the Internet on your Galaxy S10.

If you want a little more understanding as to why there are multiple options, read the nearby sidebar on Internet terminology.

For your purpose, tap either the Chrome icon or the Google icon to get started. These icons will typically be on the Home screen. Alternatively, tap the Application icon and find the Chrome or Google icon.

TIP

If you love Bing, you are not out of luck. Bing is either on your phone, or you can get it installed (I cover how to install things like Bing in Chapter 8). For now, just stay with Chrome and Google. Things on other browsers and search engines are mostly similar, and choosing the Chrome/Google pair simplifies things.

BASIC INTERNET TERMINOLOGY FOR DUMMIES

The term *Internet access* can mean a few different things. In some circumstances, the word Internet can mean a web browser. A *web browser* is an app that will display pages on the Internet. In other circumstances, the word Internet may refer to a search engine. You use a *search engine* to find either information you are seeking or to bring you to a website. Then you use a web browser to look at the information. Chances are the web browser on your phone that you will use is an app from Google called Chrome.

The chances are that the search engine you use on your phone is Google, but it may be the search engine for Microsoft called Bing. The goal with your phone is to get you where you want with minimal fuss. It is easier for the people that are bringing you this phone and service (Samsung, Google, and your wireless carrier) to give you three icons that essentially point to the same thing than to explain the terminology. Tapping the Internet icon, the Chrome icon, or the Google icon will most likely bring up the Chrome web browser.

As long as you're connected to the Internet (that is, you are either near a Wi-Fi hotspot or in an area where you have cellular service), your home page appears. If you tap the Google icon, it will be Google. If you tap Chrome, your default home page could be blank or the Google home page, but many cellular carriers set their phones' home pages to their own websites.

If you're out of coverage range or you turned off the cellular and Wi-Fi radios because you turned on Airplane mode, you get a pop-up screen letting you know that there is no Internet connection. (Read about Airplane mode in Chapter 2.)

TIP

If you should be in coverage but are not connected or when you get off the airplane, you can re-establish your connections by pulling down the Notification screen and either tapping the Wi-Fi icon at the top or turning off Airplane mode.

Accessing Mobile (or Not) Websites

The browser on your phone is designed to work like the browser on your PC. At any time, you can enter a web address (URL) by tapping the text box at the top of the screen. You can try this by typing in the address of your favorite website and seeing what happens.

For example, the page shown in Figure 7-2 is the regular version of the website Refdesk.com.

FIGURE 7-2:
The regular version of the website Refdesk.com.

As you can see, the website is all there. Also as you can see, the text is very small. This particular website is designed to take you to a lot of useful links throughout the Internet, so this is an extreme example of a regular website.

While this text is crisp and bright on your beautiful screen, it is still small. You can stretch and pinch to find the information you need. (*Stretching* and *pinching* are hand movements you can use to enlarge/shrink what you see onscreen, as covered in Chapter 2.) With a little bit of practice, you can navigate your familiar websites with ease.

The other option is to find the mobile version of a website. As a comparison, Figure 7-3 shows the mobile version of Refdesk.com. It has fewer pictures, the text is larger, and the mobile version loads faster — but it's less flashy.

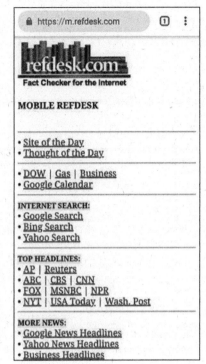

FIGURE 7-3:
The mobile version of Refdesk.com.

TECHNICAL STUFF

In the case of RefDesk, you can get to the mobile version by entering **m.refdesk. com** into the text block at the top from the software keyboard. Refdesk.com is far from the only website to offer a mobile version. Many sites — from Facebook to Flickr to Gmail to Wikipedia — offer mobile versions.

So how do you get to the mobile websites? If a website has a mobile version, your phone browser will usually bring it up without your having to do anything. Samsung has gone out of its way to work to make the web experience on the Galaxy S10 phone as familiar as possible to what you experience on your PC.

The most common difference between the address of a mobilized website and a regular one is /mobile.com at the end of the address. For example, the mobile version of Amazon.com is www.amazon.com/mobile.

If your phone doesn't automatically bring up the mobile version of a site for some reason, the simplest way to find it is to search for the desired site along with the term **mobile**. For example, the first option you get from searching for IMDb mobile on your phone is the mobilized website for the Internet Movie Database.

Choosing Your Search Engine

If you tapped one of the icons shown in Figure 7-1, you opened up the browser. Now would be a good time to try some of your favorite websites. Go ahead and tap in a few website addresses and see how they look!

One of the early goals for browsers that work on smartphones was to replicate the experience of using the Internet on a PC. For the most part, the browsers on your phone achieve that goal, even if you probably need to practice your zooming and panning.

One of the key decisions for your browser is which search engine you want as the default. You probably want whatever is the search engine that exists on your desktop PC. The leading options are all really good, but you'll probably be happiest with the search engine that you use the most. If you don't care, feel free to skip to the next section on bookmarks.

1. **From the browser screen, tap the Settings icon.**

    Tapping the Settings icon, the three vertical dots to the right of the website address, brings up the menu options shown in Figure 7-4.

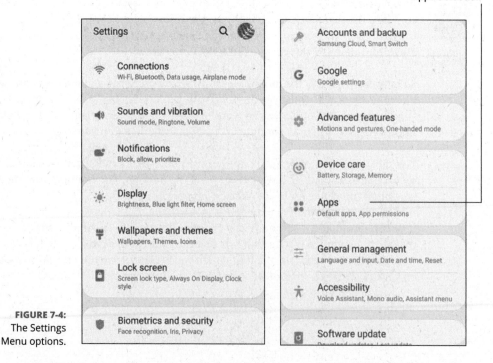

FIGURE 7-4:
The Settings Menu options.

2. Tap the Apps link.

Tapping the Apps link brings up the screen shown in Figure 7-5.

FIGURE 7-5:
The Apps screen.

3. Tap the three vertical dots on the top right.

The screen shown in Figure 7-6 appears.

Sort by size

Default apps

App permissions

Show system apps

Special access

FIGURE 7-6:
The Apps menu
pop-up.

Reset app preferences

4. **Tap the link for Default apps.**

   The screen shown in Figure 7-7 appears.

FIGURE 7-7:
The Default apps
selections.

5. **Tap the link for Browser app.**

   The screen shown in Figure 7-8 appears.

FIGURE 7-8:
The Search
Engine selections.

6. **Select the search engine you want.**

   Tapping the toggle switch by the name of the search engine you prefer takes care of it all.

Deciding Between Mobile Browsing and Mobile Apps

When you open the browser, you can use any search engine you want (for example, Bing or Yahoo!). This is a very familiar approach from your experience with PCs. However, you may get very tired of all the pinching and stretching of the screen.

Many companies are aware of this. What they have done is to develop a mobile app that provides you the same information as is available on their website that is formatted for a smartphone screen. Companies in particular will put the information from their website in a mobile app and then add some important mobile features.

For example, it is very convenient to order a custom-made pizza from the website of a national pizza chain. You can order your desired variety of crusts and toppings. The website version also offers directions to the nearest store. The mobile app can take this one step further and give you turn-by-turn directions as you drive to pick up your pizza.

This capability of providing turn-by-turn directions makes no sense for a desktop PC. This capability could make sense for a laptop, but a few laptops have GPS receivers built in. It is also too cumbersome and probably unsafe to rely on turn-by-turn directions from a laptop. It is much easier to get turn-by-turn directions over a smartphone.

This is just one example where downloading a mobile app offers a superior experience. The best part is you get to choose what works for you on your Galaxy S10.

Chapter **8**

Playing in Google's Play Store

One of the things that makes smartphones (such as the phones based on the Google Android platform) different from regular mobile phones is that you can download better apps than what comes standard on the phone. Most traditional cellphones come with a few simple games and basic apps. Smartphones usually come with better games and apps. For example, on your Galaxy S10 phone, you get a more sophisticated Contact Manager, an app that can play digital music (MP3s), basic maps, and texting tools.

To boot, you can download even better apps and games for phones based on the Google Android platform. Many apps are available for your Galaxy S10 phone, and that number will only grow over time.

So where do you get all these wonderful apps? The main place to get Android apps is the Google Play Store (sometimes simply called Google Play). You might be happy with the apps that came with your phone, but look into the Play Store and you'll find apps you never knew you needed and suddenly won't be able to live without.

In this chapter, I introduce you to the Google Play Store and give you a taste of what you find there.

Exploring the Play Store: The Mall for Your Phone

The Play Store is set up and run by Google, mainly for people with Android phones. Adding an app to your phone is similar to adding software to your PC. In both cases, a new app (or software) makes you more productive, adds to your convenience, and/or entertains you for hours on end — sometimes for free. Not a bad deal.

There are some important differences, however, between installing software on a PC and getting an app on a cellphone:

>> **Smartphone apps need to be more stable than computer software because of their greater potential for harm.** If you buy an app for your PC and find that it's unstable (for example, it causes your PC to crash), sure, you'll be upset. If you were to buy an unstable app for your phone, though, you could run up a huge phone bill or even take down the regional cellphone network. Can you hear me now?

>> **There are multiple smartphone platforms.** These days, it's pretty safe to assume that computer software will run on a PC or a Mac or both. On the other hand, because of the various smartphone platforms out there, different versions within a given platform aren't always compatible. The Play Store ensures that the app you're buying will work with your version of phone.

Getting to the Store

You can access the Play Store through your Galaxy S10 phone's Play Store app or through the Internet. The easiest way to access the Play Store is through the Play Store app on your Galaxy S10 phone. The icon is shown in Figure 8-1.

FIGURE 8-1:
The Play Store icon.

TIP

If the Play Store app isn't already on your Home screen, you can find it in your Apps list. To open it, simply tap the icon.

When you tap the Play Store icon, you're greeted by the screen looking something like what is shown in Figure 8-2.

Subcategories

Top-level categories

Google Play menu button

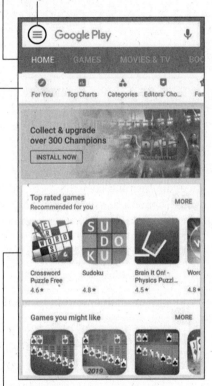

FIGURE 8-2:
The Play Store
home page.

Curated categories

As new apps become available, the highlighted apps will change, and the Home page will change from one day to the next.

In addition, the good folks at Google spend a lot of time thinking about what is the best way to help the hundreds of millions of Android users find the best application from the selection of 3.5 million apps.

This is no small task. Some of those users are very experienced and know just what they want. Others are walking in the door for the first time while still others are just coming to browse and see whether anything strikes their fancy.

The goal for Google is to make every user who comes in find what they want. The goal in this book is to give you enough information so that you can be comfortable downloading your first app and then comfortable finding other interesting apps as you become more familiar with the layout.

Seeing What's Available: Shopping for Android Apps

The panorama that exists for the Google Play home page seen in Figure 8-2 of is very extensive. You can swipe to the right a long way and you can swipe down dozens of levels. Take a look at the structure of Figure 8-2.

TIP

Do not be surprised if you open up the Play Store home page one day and find that it has a completely different layout. Google tries different formats from time to time to solve one problem or another and keep things fresh. The chances are good that the lower level categories are still there, and you can find what you are looking for, even if the structure described in this chapter is no longer exactly accurate.

Figure 8-2 shows several top-level categories (plus a few more that are off to the right):

>> **Home:** This is a catch-all category. It includes the apps for productivity, information, social connection, or enjoyment.

>> **Games:** Games are applications in which you're are an active participant. See Chapter 10 for much more information on this topic.

>> **Movies & TV:** The Google Play Store is a great source for video entertainment. Chapter 12 has more information on this subject.

>> **Music:** Likewise, the Google Play Store is a great source for audio entertainment. Chapter 12 has more information.

>> **Books:** This is the section for audiobooks and e-books. Audiobooks are the smartphone version of books on tape, where a person reads you the book. E-books allow you to use your smartphone as an e-reader.

>> **Newsstand:** This section is where you can subscribe to your favorite newspaper, magazine, or other periodical.

Navigating the Google Play home page

When you've decided that you want to look at apps, you see the following options when you tap the link for one of the top-level categories:

» **Top Charts:** These are the best-selling apps. This is often a good indication that you may want to give it a try.

» **Family:** If you're looking for apps suitable for kids, go here.

» **Categories:** This option takes you to a hierarchy of application types that is useful if you already know what you want to add. There is more on these different categories later in this chapter.

» **Editors' Choice:** While relying on sales volumes in Top Charts is one way to find apps you may find valuable, this section is curated, hopefully with people who think like you.

» **Early Access:** Let's say that you've reviewed 3.4 million apps, and you just haven't found the right one for you. You can look at the apps that have just been added to the Google Play virtual shelves by accessing this section. These are the newest apps in the store.

Google is doing its best to help you find the app you need among its inventory of hundreds of thousands of choices. Today's version of the Play Store has a link called Categories where you can start digging by app type.

» **Art & Design:** These apps let you exercise the powerful graphics process to make some cool images, from the abstract to the practical, such as floorplans.

» **Augmented Reality:** These apps give you the chance to use your camera lens and see things that are not there (in a good way).

» **Auto & Vehicles:** We love our cars. These apps help you buy them for less, enjoy them more, and enjoy them for a longer time.

» **Beauty:** These apps offer tips and techniques on how to look that much better.

» **Comics:** These apps are meant to be funny. Hopefully, you find something that tickles your funny bone.

» **Communication:** Yes, the Galaxy S10 phone comes with many communications apps, but these Play Store apps enhance what comes with the phone — for example, tools that automatically send a message if you're running late to a meeting or text you if your kids leave a defined area.

» **Dating:** This the modern way to meet that special someone, or at least someone more interesting that Saturday night TV.

» **Education:** To quote Emil Faber, "Knowledge is good."

» **Entertainment:** Not games per se, but these apps are still fun: trivia, horoscopes, and frivolous noisemaking apps. (These also include Chuck Norris facts. Did you know that Chuck Norris can divide by 0?)

» **Finance:** This is the place to find mobile banking apps and tools to make managing your personal finances easier.

» **Food & Drink:** Here is the place to find the best restaurants and obtain the best recipes.

» **Health & Fitness:** This is a category for all apps related to mobile medical apps, including calorie counters, fitness tracking, and tools to help manage chronic conditions, such as diabetes.

» **Lifestyle:** This category is a catchall for apps that involve recreation or special interests, like philately or bird-watching.

» **Maps & Search:** Many apps tell you where you are and how to get to where you want to go. Some are updated with current conditions, and others are based on static maps that use typical travel times.

» **Multimedia:** The Galaxy S10 comes with music and video services, but nothing says you have to like them. You may prefer offerings that are set up differently or have a selection of music that isn't available elsewhere.

» **News & Weather:** You'll find a variety of apps that allow you to drill down until you get just the news or weather that's more relevant to you than what's available on your extended Home screen.

» **Productivity:** These apps are for money management (such as a tip calculator), voice recording (such as a stand-alone voice recorder), and time management (for example, an electronic to-do list).

» **Reference:** These apps include a range of reference books, such as dictionaries and translation guides. Think of this section as similar to the reference section of your local library or bookstore.

» **Shopping:** These apps give you rapid access to mobile shopping sites or allow you to do automated comparison shopping.

» **Social:** These are the social networking sites. If you think you know them all, check here just to be sure. Of course, you'll find Facebook, LinkedIn, Twitter, and Pinterest, but you'll also find dozens of other sites that are more narrowly focused and offer apps for the convenience of their users.

» **Software Libraries:** Computers of all sizes come with software libraries to take care of special functions, such as tools to manage ringtones, track app performance, and protect against malware.

- » **Sports:** You can find sports sites to tell you the latest scores and analyses in this part of the Play Store.

- » **Themes:** Your phone comes with color schemes, or *themes.* This part of the Play Store offers a broader selection.

- » **Tools:** Some of these apps are widgets that help you with some fun capabilities. Others are more complicated and help you get more functionality from your phone.

- » **Travel:** These apps are useful for traveling, including handy items, such as currency translations and travel guides.

Then there are the curated categories, which change over time. The Google Play Store does its best to keep these categories fresh and customized for your needs and tastes.

TIP

The Play Store's algorithms aren't always perfect. For some reason, they keep showing me curated apps related to fashion, personal hygiene, and self-grooming. This has to be a mistake.

TIP

Many of your favorite websites are now offering apps that are purpose-built for your phone. Chapter 7 talks about how you can access websites on your phone. You can use the full site with your high-resolution screen or use the mobile version. An alternative is to download the app for that website, and it will present the information you want from that website on your phone in a way that is even easier to access. In fact, when you enter a website, your phone will look to see if you have the corresponding app. If so, you phone automatically opens the app for you. Cool!

Navigating the Google Play games page

There are lots and lots of options for entertainment in this section, which you access by tapping the Games link shown in Figure 8-2. They're categorized as follows:

- » **For You:** This is Google, so they have computers that take what they know about you so far and make a list of what may appeal to you based on that information.

- » **Top Charts:** As with apps, these are the best sellers among games. It's a good place to start.

- » **New:** This is like Early Access for apps, but for games.

>> **Premium:** These are the games that you can use for a price. Some are one-time fees; others involve ongoing charges. The benefit of paying for some game titles is that you don't have to ignore ads. In other cases, the free games offer you just a taste of what you would get, and all the really cool things are only available when you pay the piper.

>> **Categories:** This option takes you to a hierarchy of application types — useful if you already know what you want to add. I offer more info on the different categories later in this chapter.

>> **Family:** This is an entire section for games to keep the kids happy.

Your Galaxy S10 phone takes interactive gaming to a new level. Games in this section of the Play Store fall into the following categories:

>> **Arcade & Action:** Think of games that are based on what you find in arcades: shooting games, racing games, and other games of skill and/or strategy.

>> **Brain & Puzzle:** Think crossword puzzles, Sudoku, and other word or number games.

>> **Cards & Casino:** You can find an electronic version of virtually every card or casino game. (If you know of any game that's missing, let me know so that I can write the app and sell it to the three people who play it.)

>> **Casual:** This crossover category includes simpler games, some of which are also arcade, action, or cards, but are distinguished by the ease with which you can pick them up, play them, and then put them down. Solitaire may be the most widespread example of a casual game.

>> **Educational:** Who says games can't be educational, too? That would not include anyone who has browsed this section!

>> **Music:** Here are the music-based games you were looking for.

>> **Racing:** Who needs one of those game consoles to race cars when you have your S10?

>> **Role Playing:** This is the place to look if you want an immersive game that will take you to a new world.

>> **Sports:** You can find sports sites to tell you the latest scores or find you fantasy sports leagues.

>> **Strategy:** If you want to find how clever you are (or aren't), strategy games are for you. Think chess or bridge, but on your S10.

>> **Trivia:** What was the name of the high school in *Welcome Back, Kotter?* Which is larger: the moon or Pluto? If these questions capture your imagination, this is your new favorite category.

>> **Travel:** These apps are useful for traveling, including handy items, such as currency translations and travel guides.

Below the subcategories are rows of curated game categories. If you find a row that you like, you can start scrolling to the right to see the options within that curated category. Hopefully, the curator thinks like you do and can offer you lots of suggestions. This is particularly handy if you're not sure what you want.

TIP

Free apps are great. But don't be afraid of buying any apps that you're going to use frequently. Apps usually cost very little, and the extra features may be worth it. Some people (including me) have an irrational resistance to paying $1.99 monthly for something they use all the time. Frankly, this is a little silly. Let's all be rational and be willing to pay a little bit for the services we use.

Installing and Managing an Android App

To make the process of finding and downloading an app less abstract, I show you how to download and install one in particular as an example: the Facebook for Android app.

Downloading the Facebook app

Follow these steps to add this app:

1. Tap the Play Store icon.

2. In the Query box, type Facebook.

Doing so brings up a drop-down screen like the one shown in Figure 8-3.

As you can see in the search results, several options include the word Facebook. The other lines in the Apps section are for apps that include the word Facebook. These are typically for apps that enhance Facebook in their own ways — as of this moment, 112,160 of them. Rather than go through these one by one, stick with the one with the Facebook icon.

FIGURE 8-3:
The Facebook
Search results.

3. **Tap the anywhere in the box with the Facebook logo.**

When you tap the box, it brings up the screen shown in Figure 8-4.

Before continuing to the next step, I want to point out some important elements on this page:

- **Title Line:** The top section has the formal name of the app just above the green Install button. After you click this to download and install the app, you see some other options. I give some examples later in this chapter.

- **Description:** This tells you what the app does.

- **Screen Captures:** These representative screens are a little too small to read, but they do add some nice color to the page.

- **What's New:** This information is important if you have a previous version of this app. Skip this section for now.

- **Ratings and Reviews:** This particular app has about 4.1 stars out of 5. That's not bad at all. The other numbers tell you how many folks have voted, how many have downloaded this app, the date it was released, and the size of the app in MB.

- **Similar Apps:** Just in case you aren't sure about this particular app, the good folks at Google offer some alternatives.

- **More by Facebook:** The app developer in this case is Facebook. If you like the style of a particular developer, this section tells you what other apps that developer offers.

- **Based on Your Recent Activity:** Play Store tells you the names of other apps downloaded by the customers who downloaded this app. It's a good indicator of what else you may like.

- **Google Play Content:** This is how you tell the Play Store whether this app is naughty or nice.

Screen captures

Title   Rating & Review Sections (con't)

FIGURE 8-4:
The Facebook
app screen in
panorama.

Rating & Review sections

Description

4. **Tap the dark green button that says Install.**

   You see the progress of the app downloading process. When the app is all there, it begins the installation process.

   At some point in the process, most apps give you a pop-up to let you know what information from your phone that the app will use. This is to give you an idea on how this particular app may affect your privacy. An example of a permission pop-up is shown in Figure 8-5.

FIGURE 8-5:
The Facebook permissions screen.

   Chapter 1 discusses the option to prevent an app from having access to your location information. I mention that you can allow apps to know where you are on a case-by-case basis. Here is where that issue comes up. Each app asks you for permission to access information, such as your location. If you don't want the app to use that information or share it somehow, here's where you find out whether the app uses this information. You may be able to limit the amount of location information. If you're not comfortable with that, you should decline the app in its entirety.

TIP

   This is similar to the license agreements you sign when installing software on your PC. Hopefully, you read them all in detail and understand all the implications. In practice, you hope that it's not a problem if lots of other people have accepted these conditions. In the case of a well-known app like Facebook, you're probably safe, but you should be careful with less-popular apps.

   After the app downloads and installs, you will come back to a screen like the one in Figure 8-6.

5. **Tap the dark green Open button.**

   This brings up the Home screen for Facebook, as shown in Figure 8-7.

   If you have a Facebook account already, go ahead and enter your information. Things will look very familiar. If you don't have a Facebook account, and you want to add one now, go on to the next section.

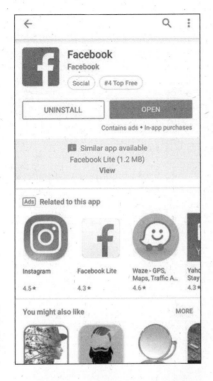

FIGURE 8-6:
The Play Store app screen for a successfully downloaded app.

FIGURE 8-7:
The Facebook login screen.

In any case, the Facebook icon appears on your Apps screen along with some other recently added apps, such as Angry Birds and Solitaire. This is seen in Figure 8-8.

REMEMBER

If you want this app to be on your Home screen, press and hold the icon. The Facebook icon appears on your Home screen.

Creating a Facebook account

If you don't already have a Facebook account, you can create an account here. Toward the bottom of the screen is the option to sign up for Facebook. Tap the Sign Up for Facebook link, and you see the screen shown in Figure 8-9.

To sign up for Facebook, you should have the following information:

>> **Name:** This would seem to be simple question. However, you should consider adding former names and/or nicknames. This all depends upon whether you want to be found by old friends or not.

>> **Mobile number:** Your mobile telephone number will auto-populate for this question. You may want to use another number. Your choice.

>> **Your birthday:** Go ahead. Tell the truth on this one.

>> **Your password:** Pick one that you can remember.

>> **Your gender:** I am not sure why Facebook needs to know this, but pick one gender.

← Terms & Privacy

Join Facebook

Create an account in a few easy steps

By signing up, you agree to our Facebook Terms and that you have read our Data Policy, including our Cookie Use. You may receive SMS Notifications from Facebook and can opt-out at any time.

Next

FIGURE 8-9:
The Sign Up for Facebook Home screen.

After you enter this information, Facebook sends a verification message. If you provide an email address, the app sends you an email. If you use your mobile phone number, it sends you a text.

The email or text contains a code. Enter this code, and your Facebook account is validated. To get the most out of Facebook, I recommend checking out *Facebook For Dummies*, 7th Edition (John Wiley & Sons, Inc.) by Carolyn Abram.

Within the Facebook app itself, you see the latest posts from your friends in an instant. You get your daily serving of cute kitten images, stories from proud parents about their children, and messages from old flames wondering about what might have been.

The Facebook mobile app is pretty popular with users. According to Facebook, more than half of Facebook users only use their smartphones and never bother to check their posts on a PC!

Rating or Uninstalling Your Apps

Providing feedback to an app is an important part of maintaining the strength of the Android community. It's your responsibility to rate apps honestly. (Or you can blow it off and just take advantage of the work others have put into the rating system. It's your choice.)

If you want to make your voice heard about an app, here are the steps:

1. **Open the Play Store.**

   Refer to Figure 8-2 to see the layout.

2. **Tap the Menu button (the three parallel lines in the Google Play banner).**

   Doing so brings up a drop-down menu like the one shown in Figure 8-10.

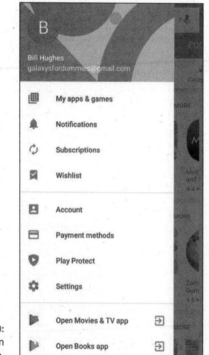

FIGURE 8-10:
The menu from
the Play Store.

3. **Tap the link that says My Apps & Games.**

   This tap brings up the screen shown in Figure 8-11, which lists all the apps on your phone. Keep on scrolling down. You'll eventually see them all.

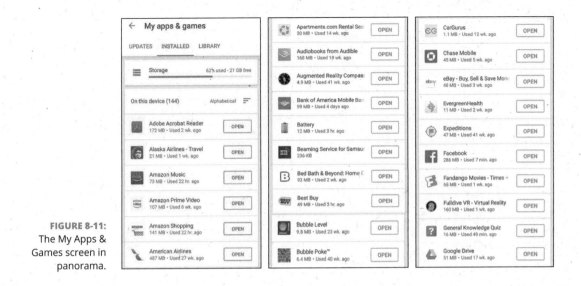

FIGURE 8-11:
The My Apps &
Games screen in
panorama.

Tapping on one of these apps is how you rate them or uninstall them, as shown in Figure 8-12.

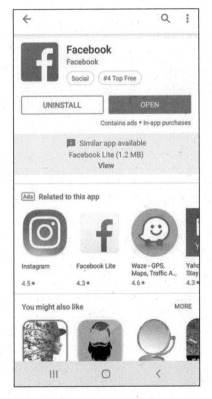

FIGURE 8-12:
The Apps page
for Facebook
after it is
installed.

If you love the app, rate it highly on a five star scale. To be clear, to rank it as one star, tap the leftmost star. To rank it highly with five stars, tap the rightmost star.

Whatever number of stars you pick will bring up a pop-up with those number of stars, as shown in Figure 8-13. You can then tell all the world just what you think of the app.

FIGURE 8-13:
The Rating
pop-up.

While many app developers read the comments, it takes longer for some. I am still waiting to hear back from my comments. Please note that seeking bribes to provide positive reviews is entirely my idea, and you should probably not copy this approach. I will sue if you do.

On the other hand, if you hate the app, give it one star and blast away. It does not happen often, but there are some major league loser apps out there. In most cases, it occurs when you have an older phone, and the apps you have assume some capabilities that are not there.

This will not happen for a long, long time with the Galaxy S10, but technology does march on. Someday in the future, your wonderful phone will be a relic, and some new apps will assume that your S10 can be operated through thought control/mind reading. Alas, your S10 phone does not have that feature (as far as you know). The new app will not seem to work right.

Go ahead and give that app one star and then tap the Uninstall button. Poof. It is gone.

4

Having Fun with Your Phone

Take pictures and video on your phone.

Peruse the games available on the Play Store and download the best ones to your phone.

Use Google Maps and the GPS in your phone to get you there and back.

Enjoy your favorite music wherever you go.

Chapter 9

Sharing Pictures

The Samsung Galaxy S10 should really be called a smartcamera with a phone. If you're like many mobile phone users, you love that you can shoot photographs and video with your phone.

You probably carry your phone with you practically everywhere you go, so you never again have to miss a great photograph because you left your camera at home.

And don't think that Samsung skimped on the camera on your Galaxy S10. In fact, they poured it on. Boasting 16 megapixels (MP) of muscle for starters, this camera is complemented with lots of shooting options. Then, depending upon your model, you have a range of additional lenses for special circumstances. After you've taken your images, you can view them on that wicked Super AMOLED screen. Samsung also includes a Gallery app for organizing and sharing. Plus, the camera can shoot stills *and* video.

It's truly amazing to consider the number of options that you have for your photographs and your videos. Samsung keeps on adding new options, filters, and ways to share these files. It would not be surprising if your phone now has more capabilities than your digital camera.

These capabilities actually cause a problem. There are so many options that it can be overwhelming. Research has shown that people fall into one of three categories: The first group tends to use the default settings. If they want to alter the image, they'd prefer to do it on their own PCs. The second group likes to explore some of the capabilities on the phone and will have some fun looking at the scenarios, but keep things within reason. The third group goes nuts with all the capabilities of the phone.

To accommodate everyone, this chapter starts with the basics. I cover how to use the camera on your phone, view your pictures, and share them online. This works for everybody.

I then focus on the most popular settings for the second group. There are some important capabilities.

For the third group, the best that can be done is to lead you in the right direction. As much as I would like to, it would be impossible to cover all the options and combinations. In my count, there are 2.43 billion possible combinations of filters, lighting, and modes. If you were to start now and take a picture every 10 seconds, you would not run out of combinations for over 700 years. This would not even include all the options for sharing these images.

Realistically, neither you nor your phone will last that long. To keep things in the realm of reality, I introduce only the most important and valuable options and go from there.

Say Cheese! Taking a Picture with Your Phone

Before you can take a picture, you have to open the Camera app. The traditional way is to simply access the Camera application from the Application list. Just tap the Camera icon to launch the app.

 Because the camera is so important, here are a few more ways to get to the Camera app. First, press the Power button twice. Boom. There it is. (If this happens to be turned off on your phone, you can toggle the Quick launch Camera in the Advanced Features within Settings.)

Next, unless you have turned off the capability for security purposes, there is a camera icon on your lock screen. If you swipe the icon across the screen, the

Camera app bypasses the security setting. You can snap away, but you can't access the photo gallery or any other files.

TIP

Here is a suggestion. If you see something suspicious, but are not ready to call 911, go ahead and start taking photos of what concerns you. If you need to, you can go back to the lock screen and slide the phone icon to the right to call 911, again without needing to unlock.

A closely related application on your phone is the Gallery, which is where your phone stores your images. The icons for these two apps are shown in the margin.

With the Camera app open, you're ready to take a picture within a second or two. The screen becomes your viewfinder. You see a screen like the one shown in Figure 9-1.

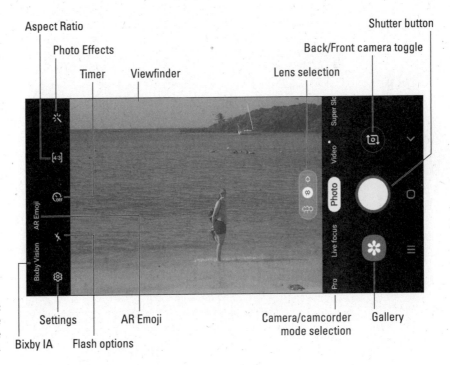

FIGURE 9-1:
The screen is the viewfinder for the Camera app.

And how do you snap the picture? Just tap the big white button on the right, which is the digital shutter button. The image in your viewfinder turns into a digital image.

A SUPER-FAST PRIMER ON SUPER AMOLED

All Samsung Galaxy S10 phones have a Super AMOLED screen. Allow me to take a moment to explain what makes this so good — and what makes you so smart for having bought the Samsung Galaxy S10.

To start, think about a typical LCD screen, like what your TV or PC might have. LCDs are great, but they work best indoors where it's not too bright. LCDs need a backlight (fluorescent, most commonly), and the backlight draws a fair amount of power, although much less power than a CRT. When used on a phone, an LCD screen is the largest single user of battery life, using more power than the radios or the processor. Also, because of the backlight on an LCD screen, these screens display black as kinda washed-out, not a true black.

The next step has been to use light-emitting diodes (LEDs), which convert energy to light more efficiently. Monochrome LEDs have been used for decades. They are also used in the mongo-screens (jumbotrons) in sports arenas. Until recently, getting the colors right was a struggle. (Blue was a big problem.) That problem was solved by using organic materials (*organic* as in carbon-based, as opposed to being grown with no pesticides) for LEDs.

The first organic LEDs (OLEDs) looked good, drew less power, and offered really dark blacks, but still had two problems. Their imaging really stank in bright light, even worse than did LCD screens. Also, there was a problem with *crosstalk* — individual pixels would get confused, over time about whether they were on or off. You'd see green or red pixels remaining on-screen, even if the area was clearly supposed to be dark. It was very distracting.

The solution to the pixels' confusion is called *Active Matrix*, which tells the pixels more frequently whether they are to be on or off. When you have Active Matrix technology, you have an Active Matrix Organic LED, or AMOLED. The image you get with this technology still stinks in bright light, but at least it's some improvement.

Enter the Super AMOLED technology, made by Samsung. When compared with the first AMOLED screens, Super AMOLED screens are 20 percent brighter, use 20 percent less power, and cut sunlight reflection by 80 percent. This is really super!

This screen still uses a significant share of battery life, but less than with earlier technologies. With Super AMOLED, you even save more power if you use darker backgrounds where possible. A few picture–taking options are right there on the viewfinder. Going from the viewfinder clockwise around the screen, the options include

>> **The viewfinder:** The viewfinder shows what will be in the picture. Okay, this is obvious, but this is also one way you control the magnification. From within the viewfinder, you can zoom in and out by pinching or stretching the screen. See Figure 9-2 for an example.

- Stretch the screen to zoom in.

- Pinch the screen to zoom out.

>> **Lens Selection:** You can zoom in by stretching or zoom out by pinching. Or you can tap one of the lens options. In Figures 9-1 and 9-2, the single tree is a telephoto with 2x magnification, the two trees are normal with 1x magnification, and the three trees are for the macro lens. Here's where there is a difference among the Galaxy S10 models. There are a different number of front and back lenses based upon the model you have and whether you're using the back- or front-facing camera. You'll see a different number of options based upon the lenses you have. This is where the extra cost pays off if you have an S10+.

FIGURE 9-2:
The viewfinder when zooming.

- >> **Rear-facing camera to front-facing camera toggle:** This icon takes you from the 16MP rear-facing camera to the not-too-shabby 10MP front-facing camera. This is a good option for selfies because you can see what the shot will look like before you snap it.

- >> **Shutter button:** This icon takes the picture.

- >> **Gallery:** Tap this icon to see the pictures you've just taken. I discuss the Gallery in the section "Managing Your Photo Images," later in this chapter.

- >> **Camera/Camcorder Mode:** These are important. Figures 9-1 and 9-2 are set for Photo mode, which is probably the best place to start. Your camera is super-smart, and Photo mode does a good job of guessing how to make your image look its best. However, if you want to get a little fancy — or really fancy — you can change the settings. You can find more on this option later in this chapter. This is also how you switch to recording video. Again, more on this later.

- >> **Settings:** Settings also gives some fancy options that are covered in the next section.

- >> **Bixby:** Bixby can do some cool things with your image. It can tell you what you're looking at. If you know what it is and want to buy it, Bixby can tell you how much it is at other retailers. More about Bixby in Chapter 14.

- >> **Flash options:** Even if you want to keep it simple, you'll want to know how to control your flash. Sometimes you need a flash for your photo. Sometimes you need a flash for your photo, but it's not allowed, as when you're taking images of fish in an aquarium, newborns, or some animals. (Remember what happened to King Kong?) Regardless of the situation, your phone gives you control of the flash. Tap the Settings icon at the top of the viewfinder. The options are Off, On, or Auto Flash, which lets the light meter within the camera decide whether a flash is necessary. The options are shown in Figure 9-3.

- >> **AR Emoji:** This option is strictly for fun! When you take a picture of someone, this options creates a cartoon-like image, called an *emoji,* of the person in the photo that you can share to show all kinds of emotions. More on this in Chapter 16.

- >> **Timer:** This creates a few second lag between the time you press the shutter button and when it takes the image so you have time to get into a group picture.

Flash always off   Flash always on

FIGURE 9-3:
Flash options.

The Galaxy S10 will figure out if
a flash is needed

>> **Aspect Ratio:** The standard photo is typically 4 units wide by 3 units high. This means that it has a 4:3 aspect ratio. This is conventional, but why be conventional all the time? You can play with different options.

>> **Camera/Video camera switch:** This icon takes you from the camera to the video camera.

FOR SKEPTICS ONLY

If you've ever used a cameraphone, you might be thinking, "Why make such a big deal about this camera's phone? Cameraphones aren't worth the megapixels they're made of." Granted, in the past, many cameraphones weren't quite as good as a digital camera, but Samsung has not only addressed these issues with the Galaxy S10, you may as well try to sell your digital camera at a garage sale because your S10 takes much better shots:

- **Resolution:** The resolution on most cameraphones was lower than what you typically get on a dedicated digital camera. The Galaxy S10, however, sports a 16MP camera — and that's good enough to produce an 8 x 10-inch print that's indistinguishable from what you could produce with a film camera, and 4 x 6-inch photos are plenty large for most uses.

- **Low Light:** Many cameraphones perform badly in low light conditions. The Galaxy S10 has an f/1.5 or f/2.4 lens, which will impress the folks who know what that means. The implication is that the S10 works incredibly well in low light.

- **AutoFocus and artificial intelligence:** We amateurs like it when a camera will do the hard work of focusing. The technology in the S10 takes a big leap by having more pixels figuring out where to focus, and then there are the smarts to figure out how to get the most out of what you see in the viewfinder.

- **Photo transfer:** With most cameraphones, the photos are hard to move from the camera to a computer. With the Samsung Galaxy S10, however (remember: it uses the Android operating system), you can quickly and easily send an image, or a bunch of images, anywhere you want, easily and wirelessly.

- **Screen resolution:** In practice, many cameraphone users just end up showing their pictures to friends right on their phones. Many cameraphone screens, however, don't have very good resolution, which means your images don't look so hot when you want to show them off to your friends. The good news is that the Samsung Galaxy S10 has a bright, high-resolution screen. Photos look really good on the Super AMOLED screen.

- **Organization:** Most cameraphones don't offer much in the way of organizational tools. Your images are all just there on your phone, without any structure. But the Samsung Galaxy S10 has the Gallery application that makes organizing your photos easier. It's also set up to share these photos easily.

TIP

You probably know that it's not a good idea to touch the lens of a camera. At the same time, it's practically impossible to avoid touching the lenses on your Galaxy S10. This can create a problem where there can be a buildup of oil and dirt on your high-resolution lens. You should clean the lens of your camera from time to time with a microfiber cloth to get the most out of your camera. Otherwise, your high-resolution images might look like you live in a perpetual fog bank.

After you take a picture, you have a choice. The image is automatically stored in another application: the Gallery. This allows you to keep on snapping away and come back to the Gallery when you have time. I cover the Gallery application more in the upcoming section "Managing Your Photo Images".

However, if you want to send that image right away, here's what you do:

1. From the viewfinder screen, tap the Gallery icon.

The viewfinder shows the Gallery icon at the top-right corner of the viewfinder. When you tap it, it brings up the Gallery application, as shown in Figure 9-4.

This brings up the current image, along with the some other recent photos.

FIGURE 9-4:
The Gallery app.

2. **Tap the thumbnail of the image you want to share.**

   It also brings up some options, as seen in Figure 9-5. Right now, you're interested in the Share option.

FIGURE 9-5:
Gallery options
for the current
image.

Share Icon

3. **Tap the Share button.**

   This brings up the options you can use to forward the image; see Figure 9-6 (although your phone might not support all the options listed here and may have a few others not in this image).

   - **Facebook:** You can take a picture and post it on your Facebook account with this option.

   - **Bluetooth:** Send images to devices, such as a laptop or phone, linked with a Bluetooth connection.

   - **Messaging:** This allows you to send it immediately to someone's phone as a text message.

- **Email:** Send the image as an attachment with your primary email account.

- **Gmail:** If your main email is with Gmail, this option and the Email option are the same.

- **Your cloud provider:** Figure 9-6 shows Goggle Drive, but if you sign up for any of the cloud storage options, they'll be here.

- **Wi-Fi Direct:** Talk about slick! This option turns your phone into a Wi-Fi access point so that your Wi-Fi–enabled PC or another smartphone can establish a connection with you.

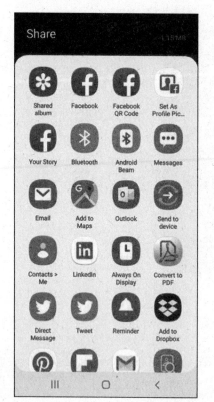

FIGURE 9-6:
Sharing options for the current image.

The point is that there is an overabundance of options. If an app on your device works with images, this is the place you can upload that image. If one of these options doesn't quite suit your need to share your pictures, perhaps you're being too picky!

Getting a Little Fancier with Your Camera

Using the default Camera settings, Photo, to snap pics is perfectly fine for those candid, casual, on-the-go shots — say, friends in your living room. However, your Samsung Galaxy S10 phone camera can support much more sophisticated shots. Your digital SLR camera has a bigger lens than your phone, but I can assure you that your phone has a much bigger brain than your camera. I suggest that even the users who want these default settings get familiar with the camera's Mode settings. These are easy to access and will improve the image quality with minimal effort.

The Photography Mode settings

The Mode setting is where you make some basic settings that describe the situation under which you will be taking your shot. The default is a single picture in Automatic mode. The Camera Effects icon is the leftmost round dot toward the bottom of the viewfinder.

Sliding this icon to the right brings up the options shown in Figure 9-7.

FIGURE 9-7:
The Photography
Mode options on
the camera
viewfinder.

The options on the left of the viewfinder bring up a number of choices:

>> **Food:** This takes pictures that emphasize the colors in food to make your friends even more jealous (and/or hungry).

- » **Panorama:** This setting lets you take a wider shot than you can with a single shot. Press the Camera button while you rotate through your desired field of view. The application then digitally stitches the individual photos into a single wide-angle shot.

- » **Pro:** This mode gets you to all kinds of camera settings that someone who knows what he or she is doing would want to control rather than let the camera make the choice. This includes setting the exposure, shutter speed, ISO sensitivity, white balance, focal length, and color tone. If you don't know what these mean, this is not the mode for you.

- » **Live focus:** This setting lets you get within 20 inches of an object, which is too close for the normal autofocus. On top of that, you can change the focus after taking the photo. (You read that right!)

- » **Photo:** Taking a single photo at a time is the default setting, which assumes average light. It's a good place to start. It's also a good place to stay most of the time.

- » **Video:** This is how you take videos with your phone. More on this option later in this chapter.

- » **Super slow-mo:** This switches you to video mode to slow down really fast shots. The exceptional thing is that your S10 does this is in full 4K resolution, so you're getting both high speed and high resolution with no compromise!

- » **Slow motion:** This is plain-old, boring slow motion. It's still cool.

- » **Hyperlapse:** You can use this setting to create a time-lapse video. The video camera will adjust the speed of the shots based upon the movement of the phone.

Choose the option that sounds right by flicking through the options, and snap away.

Settings options on the viewfinder

Tapping the Settings icon on the viewfinder brings up a number of choices. This list gives you control of the rear camera lenses, the front-facing camera lenses, which is used for selfies or video-calls, and settings that affect both cameras. These options are shown in Figure 9-8:

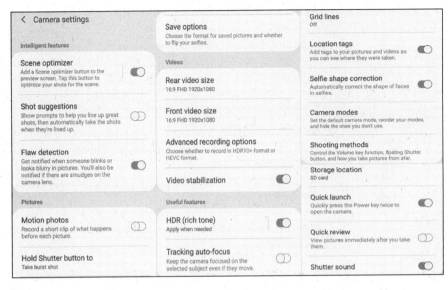

FIGURE 9-8:
The Settings
options.

>> **Scene Optimizer:** Once again, I will point out that your phone is super-smart. This setting automatically adjust setting to take the best possible picture. You can turn off this option, but why would you want to?

>> **Shot Suggestions:** This takes the scene optimizer one step further. You phone will suggest how to set up the shot, and when it's perfect, it will take the picture for you. Try it and see if you like this one.

>> **Flaw Detection:** Do you have that one relative who always seems to have his eyes closed in family photos? This capability will warn you about that problem before everyone scatters.

>> **Motion Photos:** If you select this option, your phone will record and store video just before you take the shot.

>> **Hold Shutter Button To:** You have three options here. The default when you hold down the shutter button is to take a quick series of pictures. That way, you can go back and pick the best one to keep. You could also set it so that you just take a single picture when you press and hold. Some of us are used to holding down the shutter button on an analog camera; this is the option for us. The last option is that holding down the shutter button will store the image as a GIF. If you don't know what a GIF is, you probably don't want to bother with this option.

>> **Save Options:** Your average smartphone will save your photo is one of the popular photo formats. But this isn't your average smartphone. You can change the default option to High Efficiency (HEIF) to save some storage. You can select RAW copies if you have super-duper photo-editing software back

on your PC. A third option is to save your pictures as previewed. This option is useful if you don't want to save your selfies in a format so that the lettering on your T-shirt is a mirror image (give it a try to see what I mean). Finally, the ultra-wide lens on your S10 or S10+ will distort your image. This option corrects for that effect that can makes a svelte person appear to have the physique of Homer Simpson. (Doh!)

» **Video Size:** You have the option to get really carried away here. The lowest video option is HD. HD is the minimally acceptable resolution for thoroughly modern folks. However, your phone scoffs at this puny resolution, and can take it to higher settings, as seen in Figure 9-9. The only reason to hesitate to use these higher settings is that, just as with still pictures, videos recorded in higher resolutions take more memory. It is good to know these resolutions are there. You also have the ability to set different setting for the front and back camera.

< Rear video size

● 16:9

    Resolution
    FHD 1920x1080

○ Full
    19:9 2288x1080

○ 1:1
    1:1 1440x1440

FIGURE 9-9:
Your phone's camcorder resolution options for rear and front-facing cameras.

TIP

The main consideration for SD cards has been their rated capacity. When you use your phone for video recording at standard resolution and with the standard frame rate, you're probably fine with a standard SD card. If you want a higher resolution or higher frame rate, you should get a card designed for faster data speeds. These days, the SD card is typically faster and is branded with "SDXC," but if you're using an older SD card from even a few years ago, it may choke on too much data. The solution is easy: Buy a new SD card that says SDXC.

» **Advanced Recording Options:** The Samsung Galaxy S10 can let you get really carried away with these options. You can, in spite of having gobs of storage, choose to use the high-efficiency option. You can also use HDR10+, which plays with contrast levels. Unless you know that this option is for you, you probably can skip it.

>> **Video Stabilization:** Unlike the Advanced Recording Options, this is one that you'll want. This sophisticated tool automatically makes you look like a professional videographer. When you move the camera, this option smooths out the motion. You could have just had two triple espressos, and the video will come out with smooth graceful transitions across the panorama. My advice is to leave this option on.

>> **HDR (Rich Tone):** The camera can apply this image enhancement when it's needed. You can also just leave it on all the time. Your choice.

>> **Tracking Auto-Focus:** The Samsung Galaxy S10 can spot a person's face and assumes that you want it to be the place where you focus if you toggle this option to the On position. Otherwise, if you don't use this mode, the camera may assume that you want whatever is in the center of the viewfinder to be in focus.

>> **Grid lines:** Some people like to have a 3 x 3 grid on the viewfinder to help frame the shot. If you are one of these people, toggle on this option.

>> **Location tags:** The Samsung Galaxy S10 uses its GPS to tell the location of where you took the shot. If this is too intrusive, you can leave out this information on the image description.

>> **Selfie Shape Correction:** Some selfies may distort the faces of your friends. Your Samsung Galaxy S10 can automatically fix that problem.

>> **Shooting Methods:** Do you remember the options you have for taking pictures and videos (refer to Figure 9-7)? Well, you can select them here, too. However, the default is that, when you close the camera, it will default back to Photo mode. If you want it to keep the last mode you used (say, to take videos), you can tell it to keep the last mode.

>> **Quick Launch:** You can launch the camera by pressing the Home button twice. If you would rather not, here is where you can disable that setting.

>> **Quick Review:** Some people want to see the shot right away. Others want to take a bunch of pictures and look at them at their leisure. If you want to see the image right away to see whether you need to take a second picture, turn on this toggle. It will jump you in to the Gallery app right away.

>> **Shutter sound:** It can be satisfying to hear the click when you take a picture. If you would rather not, turn that sound off here.

Photo Effects options

When you slide the rightmost dot within the viewfinder to the left, you get to see a number of effects that you can apply to your image. Some examples are shown in Figure 9-10.

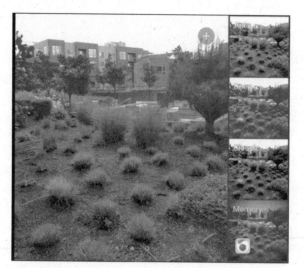

FIGURE 9-10:
Some examples
of Effects options.

Select the option that looks right for your creative vision by tapping on the thumbnail and snap away.

The Digital Camcorder in Your Pocket

Your Samsung Galaxy S10 Camera application can also function as a digital camcorder.

Starting the camcorder

All you need to do to use your phone as a video recorder is to put your camera into Camcorder mode. From the camera viewfinder, you tap the icon that looks like the record button of a movie camera in the upper-right corner, and you switch from photographer to videographer.

At this point, recording video automatically starts. You get the notification that says "Rec" in red and the timer from when it started.

The recording continues until you either tap the stop button, which is the circle with the dark square in the center on the right side of the viewfinder (see Figure 9-11), or the pause button, which is the button with the parallel slashes in the middle. If you press the upper button, the one with the silhouette of a camera, the screen will revert back to the still camera.

FIGURE 9-11:
Your phone's camcorder viewfinder.

If you press the pause button while in camcorder mode, the buttons to the bottom right morph into the options seen in the small image below it. You can tap it again to return to the video. You can also tap the shutter button to stop or tap the upper button to switch back to the camera.

REMEMBER

Your phone is not only recording the video; it's also recording the sound. Be careful what you say!

Taking and sharing videos with your camcorder

Just as you share photos you take with the camera, you can immediately share a video, play it, or delete it by tapping the video viewer. Also, the video is immediately saved on your camera. It's stored in the Gallery app or is viewable from your Video Player app (see Chapter 12).

You can get fancy with some of the settings for your camcorder, but you won't find nearly as many settings as you have for your camera (fortunately!). Two settings: AF and brightness. AF lets you changes where you want the camera to use its autofocus. The default for automatic focusing is to assume that you want whatever is smack-dab in the center of the screen to be in most focus. However, sometimes you may want to get fancy with framing the shot, and focus on your family in the bottom part of the image with Mount Rushmore taking up most of the screen. In this case, you tell the camera to autofocus on the lower part of the screen and do its best on the rest of the image. Brightness lets you adjust the brightness of the video. Otherwise, it's all automatic.

Managing Your Photo Images

After you take some great pictures, you need to figure out what to do with them. Although you can send an image immediately to another site or via email, it will likely be the exception.

In most cases, it's easier to keep on doing what you were doing and go back to the Gallery application when you have some time to take a look at the images and then decide what to do with them. Your choices include

>> Store them on your phone within the Gallery app.

>> Transfer them to your PC to your photo album application by sending them with email.

>> Store them on an Internet site, like Google Photo or Flickr.

>> Print them from your PC.

>> Email or text them to your friends and family.

>> Any combination of the preceding choices.

Unlike many regular phones with a built-in camera, the Galaxy S10 makes it easy to access these choices. You need to determine the approach you want to take to keep your images when you want them to stick around. The rest of this chapter goes through your options.

REMEMBER

Even though the Camera application and the Gallery application are closely related, they are two separate apps. Be sure that you keep straight which application you want to use.

The Gallery Home screen (refer to Figure 9-4) shows how the app first sorts the images on your phone into folders, depending upon when they originated.

All your photos from the Camera app are placed in files sorted by date. The application takes a shot at grouping them when a series of pictures or videos are taken about the same time.

Using Images on Your Phone

In addition to sharing photos from your camera, your Galaxy S10 phone allows you to use a Gallery photo as wallpaper or as a photo for a contact. And if the fancy shooting settings in the Camera application aren't enough, you can wrangle minor edits — as in cropping or rotating — when you have an image in the Gallery application.

The first step is to find the image that you want in Gallery. If you want to do something to this image other than send it, tap the Edit button at the bottom of the screen (refer to Figure 9-5). Some of the options include

» **Slideshow:** This displays each of the images for a few seconds. You can not only set the speed for transition, but also add music and select among several image transitions.

» **Crop:** Cut away unnecessary or distracting parts of the image. The application creates a virtual box around what it considers to be the main object. You can move the box around the image, but you cannot resize it. You then can either save this cropped image or discard.

» **Set As:** Make this image your wallpaper or set it as the image for a contact.

» **Print:** This option allows you to print if you have set up a local printer to communicate with your phone either through Wi-Fi or Bluetooth.

» **Rename:** These options allow you to rotate the image right or left. This is useful if you turned the camera sideways to get more height in your shot and now want to turn the image to landscape (or vice versa).

» **Details:** See the information on the image — its metadata, which is fixed and cannot change.

Deleting Images on Your Phone

Not all the images on your phone are keepers. In fact, you may get accustomed to deleting far more pictures than you keep. This is hard for some of us who are used to expensive film. However, before too long, you'll have far too many pictures, which defeats the purpose.

When you want to get rid of an image, press and hold the image you want to delete. In a second, a checkbox with the image selected will appear. Also, the links appear at the top to either Share or Delete. If you want to delete this image, tap Delete. The camera verifies that this is your intent. After you confirm, the image goes away.

If you want to delete more images, you can tap all the images you want to make go away. It is selected if it has a green checkmark on the image. Tap away, then hit delete. It will confirm with you once. Tap again and these images are gone forever.

WARNING

When I say that the photos you delete are gone forever, I do mean *for-ev-er*. Most of us have inadvertently deleted the only copy of an image from a PC or a digital camera. That's not a pleasant feeling, so be careful.

Chapter **10**

Playing Games

G ames are the most popular kind of download for smartphones of all kinds. In spite of the focus on business productivity, socializing, and making your life simpler, games outpace all other application downloads. To this point, the electronic gaming industry has larger revenues than the movie industry — and has for several years!

We could have a lively and intellectually stimulating debate on the merits of games versus applications. For the purposes of this book, the differences between games and apps are as follows:

» If a person likes a game, he or she tends to play it for a while, maybe for a few weeks or even months, and then stops using it. A person who likes an app tends to keep on using it.

» Games tend to use more of the graphical capabilities of your phone.

» People who use their phones for games tend to like to try a wide range of games.

The fact of the matter is that your Samsung Galaxy S10, with its large Super AMOLED screen and beefy graphics processing unit, makes Android-based games more fun. And because you already have one, maybe you should take a break and concentrate on having fun!

The Play Store Games Category

Chapter 8 introduces the Play Store, shown in Figure 10-1. The top level splits offerings into a few categories: Home, Games, Movies & TV, and a few other categories off to the right.

Game Home Page

FIGURE 10-1:
The Play Store
Home screen.

We want games. Games that test our skills; games that are fun; games that are cute; games that immerse us in an alternate universe! To get there, tap on the Games button!

This brings up the Games page as shown in Figure 10-2.

This section of the store has nothing but games. This section includes everything from simple puzzles to simulated violence. All games involve various combinations of intellect, skill (either cognitive or motor), and role-playing. Let's do it.

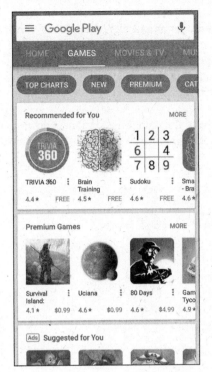

FIGURE 10-2:
The Games link
on the Google
Play Home
screen.

The Games Home screen

If you scroll around this screen, you see many suggested games. This is shown in panorama in Figure 10-3.

FIGURE 10-3:
The Games Home
screen in
Panorama.

If you aren't sure what games you might like to try, don't worry: There are lots of options. As you can see, the Games Home screen makes lots of suggestions. Each row takes a different perspective on helping you find a new game. A few of these are board games, strategy games, and action games. They also include games that allow you to play offline without Wi-Fi.

Another approach is to choose the Categories options, shown partially in the top right in Figure 10-2. This will bring up the game categories shown in Figure 10-4.

FIGURE 10-4:
The Games
Categories tab.

The Games Categories tab

In the Play Store, games are divided into the following genres:

>> **Action:** Games that involve shooting projectiles that can range from marsh-mallows to bullets to antiballistic missiles. They also involve fighting games with every level of gore possible.

>> **Adventure:** Games that take you to virtual worlds where you search for treasure and/or fight evil. Zombies and vampires are traditional evildoers.

>> **Arcade:** Game room and bar favorites.

>> **Board:** Versions of familiar (and some not-so-familiar) board games.

>> **Card:** All the standard card games are here.

>> **Casino:** Simulations of gambling games; no real money changes hands.

>> **Casual:** Games that you can easily pick up and put aside (unless you have and addictive personality).

>> **Educational:** Enjoyable games that also offer users enhanced skills or information.

>> **Music:** Includes a wide range of games that involve music in one way or another. These games may include trivia, educational games involving learning music, or sing-a-long songs for kids.

>> **Puzzle:** Includes games like Sudoku, word search, and Trivial Pursuit.

>> **Racing:** Cars, go-karts, snowboards, jet skis, biplanes, jets, or spacecraft competing with one another.

>> **Role Playing:** In a virtual world, become a different version of who you are in real life, be it for better or worse.

>> **Simulation:** Rather than live in the virtual world of some game designer, create and manage your own virtual world.

>> **Sports:** Electronic interpretations of real-world activities that incorporate some of the skill or strategy elements of the original game; vary based upon the level of detail.

>> **Strategy:** Emphasize decision-making skills, like chess; a variety of games with varying levels of complexity and agreement with reality.

>> **Trivia:** A variety of games that reward you if you know things like the name of the family dog from the TV show *My Three Sons*. Its name was Tramp, but you knew that already.

>> **Word:** Games that are universally popular, such as Scrabble.

TIP

Many games appear in more than one category.

Each game has a Description page. It's similar to the Description page for apps, but it emphasizes different attributes. Figure 10-5 is an example Description page.

FIGURE 10-5: A Description page for Flow Free.

When you're in a category that looks promising, look for these road signs to help you check out and narrow your choices among similar titles:

>> **Ratings/Comments:** Gamers love to exalt good games and bash bad ones. The comments for the game shown in Figure 10-5 are complimentary, and the overall ranking next to the game name at the top suggests that many others are favorable.

>> **Description:** This tells you the basic idea behind the game.

>> **What's New:** This section tells what capabilities have been added since the previous release. This is relevant if you have an earlier version of this game.

>> **Reviews:** Here is where existing users get to vent their spleen if they do not like the game or brag about how smart they are for buying it ahead of you. The comments are anonymous, include the date the comment was left, and tell you the kind of device the commenter used. There can be applications that lag on some older devices. However, you have the Galaxy S10, which has the best of everything (for now).

>> **More Games by Developer:** If you have a positive experience with a given game, you may want to check that developer's other games. The More By section makes it easier for you to find these other titles.

>> **Users Also Viewed/Users Also Installed:** This shows you the other apps that other people who downloaded this app have viewed or downloaded. These are some apps that you may want to check out.

>> **Price:** As a tie-breaker among similar titles, a slightly higher price is a final indication of a superior game. And because you're only talking a few pennies, price isn't usually a big deal.

Leaving Feedback on Games

For applications in general, and games in particular, the Play Store is a free market. When you come in to the Play Store, your best path to finding a good purchase is to read the reviews of those who have gone before you. Although more than a million users have commented on Angry Birds, most games do not have that kind of following.

One could argue that your opinion would not move the overall rating for a frequently reviewed game like Angry Birds. The same cannot be said for other games.

One of the new paid games is Dungeoneers from Monsterious Games. The game description is shown in Figure 10-6.

FIGURE 10-6:
A game
description for
Dungeoneers.

REMEMBER

A Description page, before you download it to your phone, will show either the Install button or the price of the game; the feedback areas will be grayed out. The Description page after you download the game to your phone will offer the options to Open or Uninstall, and the feedback areas will be active.

In this case, Dungeoneers has been reviewed by 132 gamers, most of whom are pretty darn enthusiastic. Your opinion matters more for this game than for the heavily reviewed games. After you've downloaded and played a game, you can help make the system work by providing your own review. This section reviews the process, starting from the first screen of the Play Store, which was shown in Figure 10-1:

1. **Tap the Menu icon.**

   This brings up a pop-up menu like the one shown in Figure 10-7.

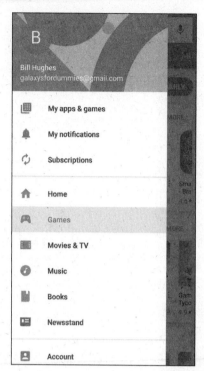

FIGURE 10-7:
The pop-up menu
for the Play Store
applications.

2. **Tap My Apps.**

This brings up the applications that you've downloaded, as shown in Figure 10-8. The Play Store does not distinguish between games and apps in this menu. They're all in the same list.

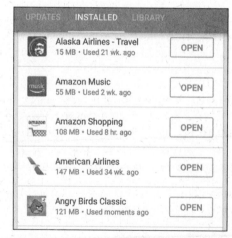

FIGURE 10-8:
Check out your
downloads.

3. **Tap the game for which you'd like to leave feedback.**

   Tapping the title of the game normally brings up the game description similar to what is shown in Figures 10-5 and 10-6. After you've downloaded a game, however, a Rate This App section appears that lets you leave feedback. See Figure 10-9 to see this section for Angry Birds.

— Review Section

FIGURE 10-9:
The Game
Description page
with space for
feedback.

4. **Tap the stars on the screen.**

   This brings up a pop-up screen, as shown on the left of Figure 10-10.

5. **Tap the number of stars you believe this game deserves.**

   The stars are between one and five. You're asked to answer some other questions that are shown in Figure 10-10, including making any comments on the last pop-up.

6. **When you're done, tap Submit.**

   Your comments are sent to the Play Store for everyone to see. For the sake of the system, make sure your comments are accurate!

FIGURE 10-10:
The ratings
stars pop-up
screen before
and after
entering
feedback.

Chapter **11**

Mapping Out Where You Want to Be

Having a map on your phone is a very handy tool. At the most basic level, you can ask your phone to show you a map for where you plan to go. This is convenient, but only a small part of what you can do.

With the right applications, your Galaxy S10 phone can do the following:

» Automatically find your location on a map.

» Give directions to where you want to go.

- As you drive, using historical driving times.

- As you drive, using real-time road conditions.

- While you walk.

- As you take public transportation.

» Give turn-by-turn directions as you travel.

- With two-dimensional representations of the road and intersections.

- With three-dimensional representations of the roads, buildings, and intersections.

>> Tell others where you are.

>> Use the screen on your phone as a viewfinder to identify landmarks as you pan the area (augmented reality).

There are also some mapping applications for the Galaxy S10 for commercial users, such as MyBusVue from Zonar Systems or Live Truck Tracking from Real Green Systems, but I don't cover them in this book.

GPS 101: First Things First

You can't talk smartphone mapping without GPS in the background, which creates a few inherent challenges of which you need to be aware. First off (and obviously), there is a GPS receiver in your phone. That means the following:

>> **Gimme a sec.** Like all GPS receivers, your location-detection system takes a little time to determine your location when you first turn on your phone.

>> **Outdoors is better.** Many common places where you use your phone — primarily, within buildings — have poor GPS coverage.

>> **Nothing is perfect.** Even with good GPS coverage, location and mapping aren't perfected yet. *Augmented reality,* the option that identifies local landmarks on the screen, is even less perfect. More about that in Chapter 14.

>> **You must be putting me on.** Your GPS receiver must be turned on for it to work. Sure, turning it off saves battery life, but doing so precludes mapping applications from working.

>> **Keep it on the down-low.** Sharing sensitive location information is of grave concern to privacy advocates. The fear is that a stalker or other villain can access your location information in your phone to track your movements. In practice, there are easier ways to accomplish this goal, but controlling who knows your location is still something you should consider, particularly when you have applications that share your location information.

REMEMBER

Good cellular coverage has nothing to do with GPS coverage. The GPS receiver in your phone is looking for satellites; cellular coverage is based upon antennas mounted on towers or tall buildings.

TIP

Mapping apps are useful, but they also use more battery life and data than many other applications. Be aware of the impact on your data usage and battery life. Leaving mapping applications active is convenient, but it can also be a drain on your battery and your wallet if you don't pay attention to your usage and have the wrong service plan.

Practically Speaking: Using Maps

The kind of mapping application that's easiest to understand is one that presents a local map when you open the application. Depending on the model of your phone, you may have a mapping applications preloaded, such as Google Maps, TeleNav, or VZ Navigator. You can find them on your Home screen and in your Application list.

It's not a large leap for a smartphone to offer directions from your GPS-derived location to somewhere you want to go in the local area. These are standard capabilities found in each of these applications.

REMEMBER

This section describes Google Maps and Google Maps Navigation; these are both free and may come preinstalled on your phone. If not, you can download them from the Google Play Store. Other mapping applications that may come with your phone, such as Bing Maps or Waze, have similar capabilities, but the details will be a bit different. Or you may want to use other mapping applications. That's all fine.

In addition to the general-purpose mapping applications that come on your phone, hundreds of available mapping applications can help you find a favorite store, navigate waterways, or find your car in a crowded parking lot. For example, Navigon and Waze offer solutions that base their navigation on real-time traffic conditions and give you turn-by-turn directions using three-dimensional images of the neighborhoods in which you are driving. For more, see the section, "Upgrading Your Navigation," at the end of this chapter.

WARNING

As nice as mapping devices are, they're too slow to tell you to stop looking at them and avoid an oncoming car. If you can't control yourself in the car and need to watch the arrow on the map screen move, do yourself a favor and let someone else drive. If no one else is available to drive, be safe and don't use the navigation service on your phone in the car.

The most basic way to use a map is to bring up the Google Maps application. The icon for launching this app is shown here.

The first screen that you see when you tap the Google Maps icon is a street map with your location. Figure 11-1 shows an example of a map when the phone user is in the Seattle area.

Map Menu   Search Box   Voice Commands

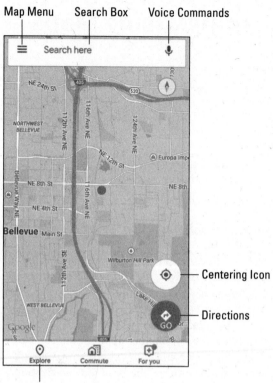

Centering Icon

Directions

FIGURE 11-1:
You start where
you are.

Local Services

Your location is the blue dot at the center of the map — unless you're moving, at which point it becomes a blue arrow. The resolution of the map in the figure starts at about one square mile. You can see other parts of the map by placing a finger on the map and dragging away from the part of the map that you want to see. That brings new sections of the map onto the screen.

TIP

Turn the phone to change how the map is displayed. Depending on what you're looking for, a different orientation might be easier.

Changing map scale

A resolution of one square mile will work, under some circumstances, to help you get oriented in an unfamiliar place. But sometimes it helps to zoom out to get a broader perspective or zoom in to find familiar landmarks, like a body of water or a major highway.

To get more real estate onto the screen, use the pinch motion I discuss in Chapter 2. This shrinks the size of the map and brings in more of the map around where you're pinching. If you need more real estate on the screen, you can keep pinching until you get more and more map. After you have your bearings, you can return to the original resolution by double-tapping the screen.

On the other hand, a scale of one square mile may not be enough. To see more landmarks, use the stretch motion to zoom in. The stretch motion expands the boundaries of the place where you start the screen. Continue stretching and stretching until you get the detail that you want. Figure 11-2 shows a street map both zoomed in and zoomed out. The map on the left is zoomed in in Satellite view. The map on the right is zoomed out in Terrain view.

FIGURE 11-2:
A street image zoomed in and zoomed out.

The app gives you the choice of Satellite view or Terrain view by tapping the menu button, the three parallel lines, on the top-left corner of the map. This brings up a pop-up menu similar to the one shown in Figure 11-3.

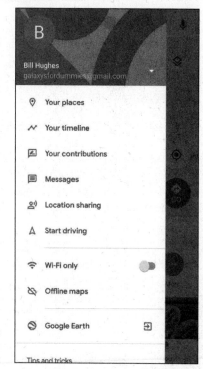

FIGURE 11-3:
The Map menu
pop-up.

Bring up the Satellite view by tapping Satellite. You get the Terrain view by tapping Terrain. You can also bring up other views that are useful to you, including transit routes and bicycling paths. I show you some of the other options in the next section in this chapter.

TIP

If you're zooming in and can't find where you are on the map, tap the dot-surrounded-by-a-circle icon (refer to Figure 11-1 for the centering icon). It moves the map so that you're in the center.

Finding nearby services

Most searches for services fall into a relatively few categories. Your Maps application is set up to find what you're most likely to seek. By tapping the Local Services icon at the bottom of the page (refer to Figure 11-1), you're offered a quick way to find the services near you, such as restaurants, coffee shops, bars, hotels, attractions, ATMs, and gas stations, as shown in Figure 11-4.

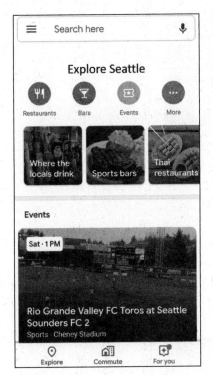

FIGURE 11-4:
Tap to find a
service on
the map.

Not only that, it is aware of the time of day. There are different suggestions during breakfast time than in the evening. Just scroll down and tap one of the topical icons, and your phone performs a search of businesses in your immediate area. The results come back as a regular Google search with names, addresses, and distances from your location. An example is shown in Figure 11-5.

In addition to the location and reviews, the search results include icons and other relevant information:

>> **Directions:** Tap the car icon to get turn-by-turn directions from your location to this business.

>> **Call:** Tap this to call the business.

>> **Save:** Tap the star to set this place as one of your favorites.

>> **Website:** Tap this to be taken to the website for this business.

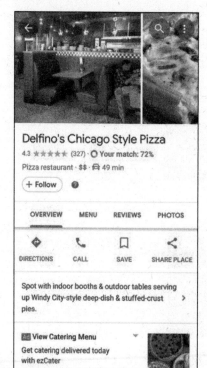

FIGURE 11-5:
The results of a service selection.

>> **Share Place:** Tap the Share Place icon, and you're presented with lots of ways to tell your friends, family, co-workers, and the world about this wonderful place.

>> More options, which include

- *Street View:* See the location in Google Street View. As shown at the bottom of Figure 11-6, Street View shows a photo of the street address for the location you entered.

- *Hours:* If this establishment has shared its hours of operation, you can find them here.

- *Menu:* If this establishment has shared its menu, you can find it here.

- *Reviews:* This includes all kinds of information about what people have experienced this location.

- *More:* Run another Google search on this business to get additional information, such as reviews from other parts of the web.

But let's say you show up, and the line is out the door. It happens. All you need to do is tap the street address, and the local map will appear as shown in Figure 11-6. This map tells you all the locations around you so you can find another option.

FIGURE 11-6:
A street map
search result.

Getting and Using Directions

You probably want to get directions from your map application. I know I do. You can get directions in a number of ways, including:

>> Tap the Search text box and enter the name or address of your location — for example, Seattle Space Needle or 742 Evergreen Terrace, Springfield, IL.

>> Tap the Explore icon (refer to Figure 11-1), tap the Attractions icon (refer to Figure 11-4), and select your location.

Any of these methods lead you to the map showing your location.

It might seem intuitive to expect that when you search for a specific attraction (such as the Seattle Space Needle), you get only the Seattle Space Needle. Such a result, however, is sometimes too simple. A given search may have multiple results, such as for chain stores. Google Map gives you several choices, and you may need to choose your favorite. Typically, the app will give you the closest option.

To get directions, tap the Directions icon. This brings up the pop-up screen shown in Figure 11-7.

FIGURE 11-7:
Your direction
options, from
original location
to the target.

This gives you the options of

>> **Driving:** Turn-by-turn directions as you drive from where you are to the destination.

>> **Public Transportation:** This option tells you how to get to your destination by taking public transportation using published schedules.

>> **Taxi or Ride Service:** This option gives the time if you were to hop a taxi, Uber, or Lyft.

>> **Cycling:** This option is for the cyclists among us; it includes bike trails in addition to city streets.

>> **Walking Navigation:** Turn-by-turn directions as you walk to your destination.

For each of these options, you can use the options at the bottom of the screen to

>> **Get Directions:** Sequential directions, as shown in Figure 11-8, but without telling you when to turn.

>> **Navigate:** Rather than show you a map, this option puts you in a navigation app that monitors where you are as you travel and tells you what to do next.

13 min (4.7 mi)
Fastest route, the usual traffic

Steps

Delfino's Chicago Style Pizza, Northeast University Village Street, Seattle, WA

Head west toward 25th Ave NE

150 ft

Turn left onto 26th Ave NE

0.1 mi

Turn left onto 25th Ave NE

0.2 mi

FIGURE 11-8:
Step-by-step directions to the target.

Upgrading Your Navigation

As a rule, free navigation applications like Google Maps Navigation have real-time updates that avoid taking you on congested routes. This is very handy, particularly in urban areas. However, if that isn't enough for you, you can also upgrade to have 3D images that provide better context for landmarks. (See Figure 11-9.)

As you can see in Figure 11-9, the 2D map is perfectly usable and accurate, but the 3D map gives you context and additional information about the buildings around you, which can give you an extra level of confidence. This comes at a small price premium. So if you frequently depend on your mapping app to get where you're going, you may find it worth your while to spend money for a paid app.

FIGURE 11-9:
Comparing 2D
navigation to 3D
navigation.

REMEMBER

Paying an extra $5 to $10 monthly feels like a lot for some of us. Keep in mind, however, that

>> This amount is relatively modest compared to what you're paying monthly for your service.

>> The price of a dedicated GPS receiver, with almost exactly the same capabilities, is between $125 and $200. The monthly cost of the service is comparable to the one-time fee of the GPS receiver. Plus, you don't have the hassle of lugging an additional device and its wiring.

TIP

Sometimes the app gives audio instructions. The Google App has a speaker icon that appears on the map that allows you to turn audio instructions on or off.

DRIVING SAFELY

Using your phone while driving is a bad idea. Texting while driving is illegal in most states, but studies have shown that laws don't affect behavior that much. It's just so darn tempting to sneak a peek at your phone. The grim reality: According to the National Highway Transportation Administration, texting while driving resulted in just under 600 deaths in the United States in 2016. When you include all the sources of distracted driving (eating, drinking, adjusting the radio, and so on), 3,450 people were killed.

To make matters worse, distracted driving is disproportionately problematic for younger drivers. You can't do much to stop your teen from checking out his hair in the rearview mirror while he's driving, but you can install an app on his phone that will prevent him from texting while the car is in motion. The simplest apps track speed — if the phone is going above some preset limit, it shuts off the phone's communication. More sophisticated apps give you more options, including the ability to place calls to 911 or a list of exceptions, a code that you can enter if you're the passenger and not the driver, and more.

If you have trouble setting down your phone, you may even want to install one of these apps for yourself *and* for your teen.

Chapter **12**

Playing Music and Videos

S martphones have built-in digital music and video players. There was a time not too long ago that having a dedicated music or video player was the way to go. However, having a single device that you can use as a phone *and* as a source of entertainment is more convenient because then you need only one device rather than two, and you eliminate extra cords for charging and separate head-phones for listening. Your Samsung Galaxy S10 is no exception. You can play digital music files and podcasts all day and all night on your phone. The audio and video technology embedded in your phone is truly among the best there is.

In addition, by virtue of the Super AMOLED screen on your Galaxy S10 smart-phone, your phone makes for an excellent handheld video player. Just listen on the headset and watch on the screen, whether you have a short music video or a full-length movie. You may look at your phone and wonder how good watching a video can be with a relatively small screen, but once you start, the screen is so good, you become immersed in no time.

To boot, your Galaxy S10 comes with applications for downloading and listening to music as well as downloading and watching videos. These apps are very straightforward, especially if you've ever used a CD or a DVD player. I will judge the success of this chapter by the number of MP3 and CD players that readers list on eBay.

Getting Ready to Be Entertained

Regardless of the model phone you have, the particular app you use for entertainment, and whether you're listening to audio or watching video, here's where I cover some common considerations up front.

The first is the use of headsets. Yeah, you used *headphones* with your MP3 player, but you probably want to use a *headset* with your phone. The vocabulary is more than just semantics; a headset has headphones plus a microphone on the cable. This makes it easier for when you get a call while listening to music or watching a movie.

Your phone sees an incoming call and will pause the music or movie and show you the caller ID. If you answer it and you have a headset, you can be reasonably assured that the person on the other line will hear you loud and clear. If you have headphones, the phone will use the built-in microphone for your voice while you hear the caller on your headphones. My advice is to test the sound quality using a headphone and judge for yourself whether you want to use a headset or headphones.

Next, I explore speakers. I touch on speakers in Chapter 3 when talking about Bluetooth pairing and in Chapter 16 when I talk about making the phone your own. As you may guess, having a solid strategy for speakers is important to get the most out of your Galaxy S10.

Then you need to know about connecting your Galaxy S10 phone to a television and/or stereo. After I talk about that, I cover the issue of licensing multimedia material.

Finally, I explore storing all these options on your phone for your offline enjoyment. You can have gobs of storage at your disposal if you want. I explore what the term "gobs" really means in terms of audio and video storage.

Choosing your headset

You can use wired or wireless (Bluetooth) headsets with your Samsung Galaxy S10 phone. Wired headsets are less expensive than Bluetooth headsets, and, of course, wired headsets don't need charging, as do the Bluetooth headsets.

On the other hand, you lose freedom of mobility if you're tangled up in wires. In addition, the battery in Bluetooth headsets lasts much longer than the battery in your phone. However, if your headset happens to be running low and it can be charged wirelessly, you can use the PowerShare feature of your S10 to extend the life of your headset until you can recharge everything.

Wired headsets

At the bottom of your Galaxy S10 phone is a headset jack. If you try to use your regular headphone jack in this jack, you'll hear the audio, but the person on the other end of the call may not hear you as well because the headphones don't come with a microphone. In such a case, your phone tries to use the built-in mic as a speakerphone. Depending upon the ambient noise conditions, it may work fine or sound awful. Of course, you can always ask the person you're talking to whether he or she can hear you.

To address that problem, your phone might come with a wired headset. In that case, just plug it in to use the device. The Galaxy S10 uses ear buds, like those shown in Figure 12-1.

FIGURE 12-1:
A typical wired headset with ear buds and a 3.5mm plug.

Some people dislike ear buds. You can obtain other styles at a number of retail franchises that offer options, including:

>> Around-the-ear headphones that place the speakers on the ear and are held in place with a clip.

>> A behind-the-neck band that holds around-the-ear headphones in place.

>> An over-the-head band that places the headphones on the ear.

WARNING

The laws in some regions prohibit the use of headphones while driving. Correcting the officer and explaining that these are really "headsets" and not "headphones" won't help your case if you're pulled over. Even if not explicitly illegal in an area, it's still a bad idea to play music in both ears at a volume that inhibits your ability to hear warnings while driving.

Ear buds can have a greater chance of causing ear damage if the volume is too loud than other options. The close proximity to your eardrum is the culprit. There are probably warnings on the ear bud instructions, but I wanted to amplify this information (<harhar>).

In any case, give yourself some time to get used to any new headset. There is often an adjustment period while you get used to having a foreign object in or around your ear.

Stereo Bluetooth headsets

The other option is to use a stereo Bluetooth headset. Figure 12-2 shows a few options.

Over the Ear
Headset

On-the-Ear
headphone

In the Ear Headset

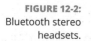

FIGURE 12-2:
Bluetooth stereo
headsets.

You need to consider a few important options before you put down your money and buy one. First, you have a choice of the earpieces being "on" the ear, "over" the ear, or "in" the ear.

The over-the-ear option tends to eliminate outside noise a little better because your ears are surrounded by the cushions. This can also get hot if you wear your headset for an extended time. On the other hand, some over-the-ear headsets have noise cancelling, which is nice in noisy areas, like airplanes.

The on-the-ear headphone is good for when you have your headphones on for a long time. The on-the-ear headphone seen in Figure 12-2 is a Bedphone that is designed specifically for use in bed, including as you sleep. How cool is that?

The third option for headsets includes those that insert into your ear canal. The ear buds in Figure 12-2 are Samsung Galaxy Buds. Although they work with any Bluetooth device, they work particularly well with your S10. When you insert them into your ear canal, they just stay there (If they don't, there are a few other silicone ear pieces that you can use to get them to fit). There are no wires and plugs. Having this kind of headset in your ear makes it less likely to shift or fall out than the other options. The in-the-ear headset shown in Figure 12-2 is well-suited for those who want to listen to music and have the ability to take calls has they exercise. How neat is that?

In each of these cases, a stereo Bluetooth headset is paired the same way as any other Bluetooth headset. (Read how to do this in Chapter 3.) When your Galaxy S10 phone and the headset connect, the phone recognizes that the headset operates in stereo when you're listening to music or videos. When you open the case in which you store the ear pieces, not only will the Galaxy Buds pair, but they'll bring up a screen called Galaxy Gear to let you fine-tune the sound quality. It's very slick!

Choosing your Bluetooth speaker

In the last few years, developers released a flurry of products known as *Bluetooth speakers.* These speakers include a range of options, some of which are a very small and convenient. Others are designed to offer excellent audio quality. Some of these speakers look cool or a very small but have poor sound quality. Check it out before your buy.

Although these speakers (which come in a range of sizes) are not as portable as the Bluetooth headset — they're a little difficult to use as you're walking down the street — they're usually pretty easy to take with you and set up when you're at a desk or in someone's living room. They also do not need a cable to make a connection and are always ready to go.

Cavalier Audio's Maverick (see Figure 12-3) is an excellent example of a high-quality Bluetooth speaker. Its list price is about $250.

If you like high-quality sound, this is the quality of Bluetooth speaker that you'd want to get. As you may have noticed, it looks very sleek. On the other hand, if you're just looking for background enjoyment, you can get a Bluetooth speaker for less than half that price.

Connecting to your stereo

Although being able to listen to your music on the move is convenient, it's also nice to be able to listen to your music collection on your home or car stereo. Your Galaxy S10 phone presents your stereo with a nearly perfect version of what went in. The sound quality that comes out is limited only by the quality of your stereo.

In addition, you can play the music files and playlists stored on your phone, which can be more convenient than playing CDs. If your stereo receiver is older, you have two choices:

» One setup involves plugging the 3.5mm jack from the cable shown in Figure 12-4 into the 3.5mm jack available on newer stereos.

When you play the music as you do through a headset, it will play through your stereo. Although each stereo system is unique, the correct setting for the selector knob is AUX.

» The other option is to acquire a Bluetooth receiver and connect that to your stereo (be sure it works at least with Bluetooth version 4.2 for the best sound). The Bluetooth receiver will connect with a 3.5mm jack or to an unused red and white plug pair, say, for the old cassette tape player you no longer have. This setup lets you walk around with your phone in your house. As long are you don't stray more than 30 feet from your stereo, the connection works great!

FIGURE 12-4:
The patch cable with 3.5mm plugs.

Newer stereo receivers recognize that cellular phones are a great place to access music. These receivers support a Bluetooth connection to your phone. If you are in the market for a new receiver, make sure that you get one with Bluetooth capability. In either case, you will be entertained. Enjoy yourself.

Licensing Your Multimedia Files

It's really quite simple: You need to pay the artist if you're going to listen to music or watch video with integrity. Many low-cost options are suitable for any budget. Depending upon how much you plan to listen to music or podcasts, or watch videos, you can figure out what's the best deal.

WARNING

Stealing music or videos is uncool. Although it might be technically possible to play pirated music and videos on your phone, it's stealing. Don't do it. If your financial circumstances do not allow you to afford to pay for your music, I suggest you listen to Internet Radio. With just a little work on your part, you can get free unlimited music and at least a low monthly fee if you want no advertising.

You can buy or lease music, podcasts, or videos. In most cases, you pay for them with a credit card. And depending upon your cellular carrier, you might be allowed to pay for them on your monthly cellular bill.

Listening up on licensing

Here are the three primary licensing options available for music files and podcasts:

>> **By the track:** Pay for each song individually. Buying a typical song costs about 79 cents to $1.29. Podcasts, which are frequently used for speeches or lectures, can vary dramatically in price.

>> **By the album:** Buying an album isn't a holdover from the days before digital music. Music artists and producers create albums with an organization of songs that offer a consistent feeling or mood. Although many music-playing applications allow you to assemble your own playlist, an album is created by professionals. In addition, buying a full album is often less expensive than on a per-song basis. You can get multiple songs for $8 to $12.

>> **With a monthly pass:** The last option for buying audio files is the monthly pass. For about $15 per month, you can download as much music as you want from the library of the service provider.

TECHNICAL STUFF

If you let your subscription to your monthly pass provider lapse, you won't be able to listen to the music from this library. This music is *streamed* through the Internet and not stored on your phone.

In addition to full access to the music library, some music library providers offer special services to introduce you to music that's similar to what you've been playing. These services are a very convenient way to learn about new music. If you have even a small interest in expanding your music repertoire, these services are an easy way to do it.

Whether buying or renting is most economical depends on your listening/viewing habits. If you don't plan to buy much, or you know specifically what you want, you may save some money by paying for all your files individually. If you're not really sure what you want, or you like a huge variety of music, paying for monthly access might make better sense for you.

Licensing for videos

The two primary licensing options available for videos are:

>> **Rental:** This option is similar to renting a video from a store. You can view the video as many times as you like within 24 hours from the start of the first play. In addition, the first play must begin within a defined period, such as a week, of your downloading it. Most movies are in the $3 to $5 range.

>> **Purchase:** You have a license to view the file as frequently as you want, for as long as you want. The purchase cost can be as low as $12, but is more typically in the $15 range.

At the moment, there are no sources for mainstream Hollywood films that allow you to buy a monthly subscription and give you unlimited access to a film library. This can change at any time, so watch for announcements.

Using the Full Capacity of Your SD Card

Your Galaxy S10 comes with at least 128GB of storage. Okay. What does that really mean?

The Android operating system is stored on some of that storage space. Plus, the apps that you downloaded are stored here. Then, there are the files that you create and use. After it is all said and done, you probably have at least 80GB available for the storage of photos, music, and videos. So how much is that, and do you need more?

The correct answer is, "Who knows?" That is about as worthless of an answer as you will find anywhere in this book. However, I can tell you how to change that response to "It doesn't matter."

Your phone has a slot in the top where you can add a microSD card, and your Android operating system can address up to an additional 512GB of storage. Okay. So how much is that?

The easiest way to describe it is by figuring out how many photos, how many songs, and how many movies fit into 1GB.

>> **300 images:** You can take about 300 images from the camera on your phone at resolution at the default settings.

>> **Ten hours of music:** If you buy an album, it will take somewhat less than a tenth of a gigabyte. The length of albums was set based upon what could be reliably imprinted on a vinyl record. That works out to be about 45 minutes and maybe a dozen songs.

>> **About one standard definition (TV-quality) movie:** Estimating the size of videos can get really variable. TV quality video is a waste of that beautiful screen. However, an hour of video that uses every pixel of resolution will take about 4GB.

Unfortunately, at this point, you need to do a little bit of math. Say that I want to watch every minute of all 529 episodes of *The Simpsons.* This would take 194 hours or about 8 days. All I need to do is buy a 256GB chip for about $50, load it up, and put it in my phone. D'oh!

You could binge-watch all the episodes of the series *Breaking Bad* in high definition on one SD card. If you want to be able to binge-watch *Breaking Bad, Game of Thrones,* and *The Walking Dead,* it would need to be stored in standard mode. Sorry.

If you are more into music than videos, you could store over 5,000 hours of music on that poor microSD Card. You could start playing music January 1 at midnight and not repeat a single track until July 27. If you splurge and get that 512GB card for $125, you can play nonstop into late February of the next year.

Keep in mind that these are rough estimates. These calculations assume there are minor attempts to reduce the size of these files. That can have a huge impact on storage needs. Let's just say that you can put a combination of images, music, and video that will keep you entertained for a very, very long time.

Enjoying Basic Multimedia Capabilities

Regardless of the version of your Galaxy S10, some basic multimedia capabilities are common across the different phones. Figure 12-5 shows the Music and Video applications.

FIGURE 12-5:
The multimedia apps on the Galaxy S10.

Your phone comes with these applications preloaded, and you might have other multimedia applications as well, depending upon your carrier. Also, some sources of music and video, such as Netflix, have their own embedded player.

Grooving with the Play Music app

The Play Music app allows you to play music and audio files. The first step is to obtain music and audio files for your phone.

Some ways to acquire music and/or recordings for your phone are:

>> Buy and download tracks from an online music store.

>> Receive them as attachments via email or text message.

>> Receive them from another device connected with a Bluetooth link.

>> Record them on your phone.

Buying from an online music store

The most straightforward method of getting music on your phone is from an online music store. You can download a wide variety of music from dozens of mainstream online music stores. The Play Store is an option. In addition to apps, it has music and video. Other well-known sites include Spotify and Amazon Music.

In addition, many more specialty or "boutique" stores provide more differentiated offerings than you can get from the mass-market stores. For example, MAQAM offers Middle Eastern music (www.maqammp3.com).

The details for acquiring music among the online stores vary from store to store. Ultimately, there are more similarities than differences. As an example of when you know what you want, what you really, really want, here's how to find and download the song "Wannabe" by the Spice Girls. I'm using Amazon Music. If you don't have Amazon Music in your Applications list, you would start by loading that app on your phone, as I describe how to do in Chapter 8. After entering your Amazon sign-in information, you see the Amazon Music Home screen, shown on the right in Figure 12-6.

Amazon MP3 sign-in screen   Amazon MP3 Music Store Home screen

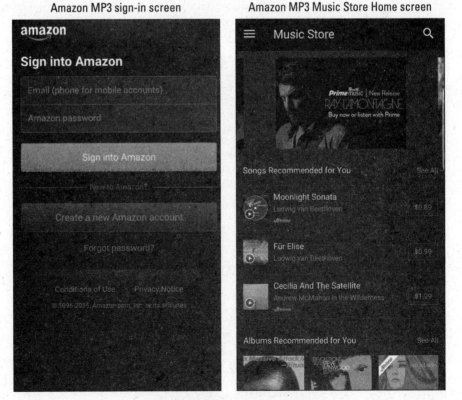

FIGURE 12-6:
The Amazon
Music login and
Home screens.

From here, you can search for music by album, song, or music genre. Now to search for the song you want:

1. **Enter the relevant search information in the Amazon Music Search field.**

   In this case, I'm searching for "Wannabe" by the Spice Girls. The result of the search for songs looks like Figure 12-7.

   The search results come up with all kinds of options, including: albums, individual tracks, similar songs, karaoke versions, and other songs from the same artist. Be ready for these options.

2. **To purchase the track, tap twice on the price.**

   The left screen in Figure 12-8 shows the price. When you tap once on the price, you get a confirmation message to make sure that you want to buy the download; the price is replaced with a Buy Song icon, as shown on the right in Figure 12-8. To buy, tap Buy Song.

3. **Expect to pay.**

   Unless you're going to subsist on the free promotional songs, you need to pay. In this case, you get the screen shown in Figure 12-9.

   The song is now loaded on your phone. When you open the music player, it's ready for you to play anytime you want to party like it's 1996!

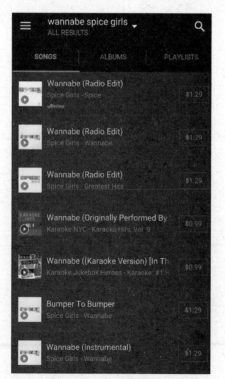

FIGURE 12-7:
Search results for a song at the Amazon Music store.

Step 1   Step 2

FIGURE 12-8:
Tap twice to buy.

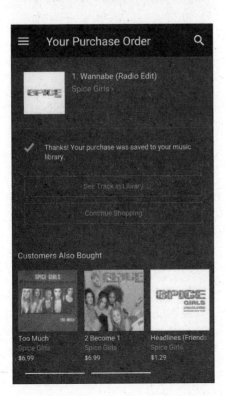

FIGURE 12-9:
The screen
confirming your
purchase from
the Amazon
Music store.

Receiving music as an attachment

As long as you comply with your license agreement, you can email or text a music file as an attachment. Simply send yourself an email from your PC with the desired music file. You then open the email or text on your phone and save the file in the library of your Music app.

Your phone can play music files that come in any of the following formats: FLAC, WAV, Vorbis, MP3, AAC, AAC+, eAAC+, WMA, AMR-NB, AMR-WB, MID, AC3, and XMF.

Recording sounds on your phone

No one else might think your kids' rendition of "Happy Birthday" is anything special, but you probably treasure it. In fact, many sound recording apps are available on your phone.

Some are basic and turn your phone into a basic voice recorder. Others can alter your voice. (I do not want to know why.) Others are meant to allow you to surreptitiously record voice conversations. Some can specifically record telephone conversations.

Be aware of privacy laws in your area! Some jurisdictions require only one party in a conversation to give permission to record a conversation. Other jurisdictions require positive consent from all parties. While rare, there have been cases where first-time offenders have spent long stints in jail for recording what was perfectly legal in another state!

In general, a simple record button creates a sound file when you stop recording. The sound quality may not be the best, but what you record can be just as important or entertaining as what you buy commercially. Your phone treats all audio files the same and all are playable on your Play Music.

Playing downloaded music

To play your music, tap the Play Music app icon shown in Figure 12-5 to open the music playing application.

Okay. Figure 12-10 shows your Home screen after your get through the initial marketing welcome. Sometimes this app can be too enthusiastic in welcoming you.

FIGURE 12-10:
Home screen
for the Play
Music app.

The first screen that you see sorts your music files into a number of categories. You can select the category you want to use by tapping on the link that says playlist. This brings up a pop-up screen.

The categories include

>> **Playlists:** Some digital music stores bundle songs into playlists, such as Top Hits from the '50s. You can also create your own playlists for groups of songs that are meaningful to you.

>> **Stations:** These are kind of like radio stations that follow a particular format. You put in a group name, like Genesis or Van Halen, and Play Music will play songs within that genre that may or may not be currently stored on your phone. Figure 12-11 shows a more recent example when I searched on Bruno Mars. The section later in this chapter on Internet Radio describes this service in more detail.

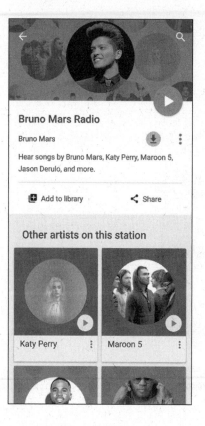

FIGURE 12-11:
Bruno Mars Radio
Station within the
Play Music app.

>> **Artists:** This category lists all songs from all the albums from a given artist.

>> **Albums:** Tapping this category places all your songs into an album with which the song is associated. When you tap the album, you see all the songs you've purchased, whether one song or all the songs from that album.

>> **Songs:** This lists all your song files in alphabetic order.

>> **Genres:** This category separates music into music genres, such as country and western or heavy metal.

These categories are useful when you have a large number of files. To play a song, an album, or a genre, open that category and tap the song, playlist, album, artist, or genre, and the song will start playing.

Adding songs as ringtones and alarms

Here's how to add a song as a ringtone or alarm. The first step is to open a contact. A generic contact in Edit mode is seen in Figure 12-12. (Refer to Chapter 6 if you have any questions about contacts.)

FIGURE 12-12: A typical contact for a Baroque composer.

Ringtone setting

Follow these steps:

1. **Tap the Default Ringtone link.**

This will bring up a list of ringtones (shown in Figure 12-13).

A quick scan finds that *Ode to Joy* is not among the options that come with your phone. To use a music file as a ringtone, find the Add button at the top.

<	RINGTONES	ADD
⦿	Default ringtone	
○	Astro	
○	Basic Bell	
○	Beep Once	
○	Beep-Beep	
○	City Lights	
○	Coffee	
○	Constellation	
○	Donkey	
○	Friday	
○	Hangouts Call	
○	Hangouts Call	
○	Hangouts Message	

FIGURE 12-13: Basic ringtones.

2. **Tap Add.**

This brings up the option to bring up the Sound Picker App. This app shows all the music files on your phone, as shown in Figure 12-14.

FIGURE 12-14:
The track
selections.

3. **Highlight the song you want and tap OK.**

   From now on, when you hear this song, you know it will be your friend Ludwig. Figure 12-15 show that this is now Ludwig's ringtone.

Jamming to Internet Radio

If you have not tried Internet Radio, you should definitely consider it. The basic idea is that you enter information on your current music favorites, and these services play music that is similar. In some stations, a great deal of research with complex statistical analysis goes into picking similar songs based upon numeric analysis of musical patterns. Other stations wing it.

The good news is that you can explore your options. Figure 12-16 shows some of the 9,000 Internet Radio apps in the Play Store. Pandora and Slacker Radio are two of the best-known services of this type; one or the other may have been preinstalled on your phone. (Actually, you may find four or more Internet Radio options preinstalled on your phone!)

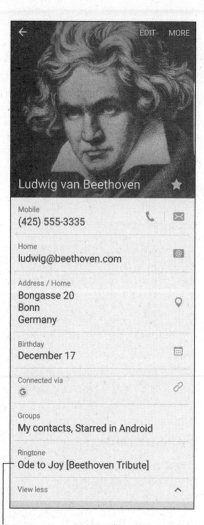

FIGURE 12-15:
The ringtone
selection.   Suitable ringtone for Ludwig

These apps are a great way to learn about new songs and groups that may appeal to you. The service streams music to your phone for you to enjoy. You can buy the track if you choose.

WARNING

Streaming audio files can use a large amount of data over time. This may be no problem if you have an unlimited (or even large) data-service plan. Otherwise, your "free" Internet Radio service can wind up costing you a lot. You're best off using Wi-Fi.

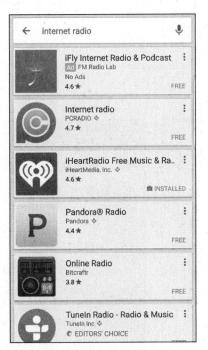

FIGURE 12-16:
Some Internet
Radio options in
the Play Store.

TIP

The selection played by even the best Internet Radio can become repetitive after a while if you listen to it enough. If you find yourself bored, do not hesitate to switch Internet Radio providers and use the same band for the radio station. This will almost always bring up new songs.

Looking at your video options

The Play Music app allows you to play music files. Similarly, you use the Video Player app to play video options. The Video Player is in your Application list and might even be on your home page. In most ways, playing videos is the same as playing audio with some exceptions:

>> Many people prefer to buy music, but renting is more typical for videos.

>> Video files are usually, but not always, larger.

Otherwise, as with music files, you can acquire videos for your phone from an online video store — and you need to have an account and pay for the use. In addition, you can download video files to your phone, and the Video Player will play them like a DVD player.

There is a great selection of videos on the Google Play Store and Amazon Prime Video. Each of these has great video selections that you can rent or buy. Figure 12-17 shows the Home screens for the Google Play Store and Amazon Prime Video.

Play Store Video Home Page

Amazon Prime Video Home Page

FIGURE 12-17:
Home screens for
Google Play Store
and Amazon
Prime Video.

Using the three screens

If you have a subscription to Amazon Video, I hereby grant you permission to watch any and all of the Amazon Video options on your Galaxy S10 (once you sign in and comply with all the terms and conditions set forth by Amazon). Once you install the Amazon Prime Video app from the Play Store, sign in with the email and password associated with your account, and all the content is there for you to stream. It is that simple. If you don't believe me, give it a try.

If you take a look at the Amazon Prime Video home page on the Internet, seen in Figure 12-18, it shows your options for access to the content to which you subscribe. The original term for this was called serving the *three screens*. Three screens referred to in the strategy included your television at home, your PC or laptop, and your smartphone.

FIGURE 12-18:
The Amazon
Prime Video
home page.

The idea is that you get one subscription and have access to the same content and, importantly, can pick up where you left off. So if you're watching a video on your television, you can pick up where you left off on your smartphone.

Amazon Prime Video is taking this one step further to ensure as many of its subscribers as possible have access. If you have a Smart TV that has an Internet connection, the chances are that Amazon Prime Video will run on the TV. If you have an old and/or a dumb TV, you can get Amazon through streaming media players, game consoles, set-top boxes, or Blu-ray players.

Amazon is not the only organization to do this. Many cable companies offer this kind of solution, as do many of the video subscription services.

The mainstream video services compete with having a broad range within their libraries that seek to appeal to as many customers as possible. Keep in mind that there are specialty video providers that offer curated videos for their subscribers.

For example, TeacherTube is a site dedicated to K-12 education, as seen in Figure 12-19. If we continue down this path further, there are a great number of options for online education. Many of these sites do not consider themselves to be video aggregators, but that's exactly what happens when they take recorded lectures and provide them to students.

The best-known online education service is the University of Phoenix. There are dozens more online universities.

Education is just one curated video service. Others exist for videos of Bollywood movies, British sitcoms, Portuguese game shows, and many other art forms.

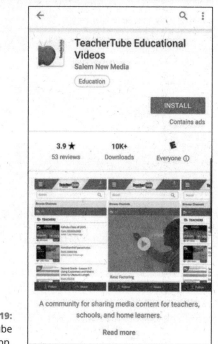

FIGURE 12-19:
The TeacherTube
app.

Viewing your own videos

In Chapter 9, I cover how to use the digital camcorder on your phone. You can watch any video you've shot on your phone. From the Google Play application, scroll over to the Personal Video section.

TECHNICAL STUFF

Your phone can show the following video formats: MPEG-4, WMV, AVI/DivX, MKV, and FLV.

To play your video, simply tap the name of the file. The app begins showing the video in landscape orientation. The controls that pop up when you tap the screen are similar to the controls of a DVD player.

The reality of virtual reality

Video games can be immersive, and a good movie can really suck you into its reality. The idea of *virtual reality* is to take this one step further. The basic idea behind virtual reality is to create a simulated world by having you wear a pair of goggles and presenting images that change the screen based upon movements of your head and body.

We can explore the concept by taking it in steps. At the most basic level, you can use your phone with a pair of *virtual reality goggles.* Samsung is offering virtual reality goggles that are designed to work with your Galaxy S10. These are seen in Figure 12-20.

FIGURE 12-20:
Samsung virtual
reality goggles.

What you do is insert your Galaxy S10 into the goggles. Then you use the little remote next to the goggles to navigate to the application. The remote is very convenient because, without it, the only way to communicate with the screen is by turning your head to commands and then holding it there for a few seconds. That little device allows you to navigate the screen while the phone is inserted in the goggles.

What happens is that your field of view is entirely taken up by the screen of your Galaxy S10. Imagine the most basic scenario, where the camera on the back of your phone shows you what is in front of you. This kind of experience is more or less comparable to using a pair of eyeglasses.

When you walk forward, things come closer. When you look down, you see the floor. When you turn your head to the right or the left, you see things that were not in your range of vision. So far, this is not very interesting.

So let's take it up a level. Now let's let your phone and all its processing capacity and intelligence tell you what you're looking at. You turn your head, and you see a picture. Presto chango, you see a little pop-up next to the picture that tells you that this is a print of Edward Hopper's *The Nighthawks.* You look out the window, and a pop-up appears with current weather conditions and a forecast for today.

Now you take your virtual reality goggles to the grocery store. As you get your cart, a familiar face comes up and starts talking. For the life of you, you cannot remember who this person is or how you know him. In just a moment, the face recognition system recognizes this person, and a pop-up identifies that this person is your old neighbor Bif Wellington. After chatting, you walk the store aisles looking for deals. You get a pop-up letting you know when this grocery is giving you a good deal on Honeycrisp apples, or if you can get them cheaper at the other store. This capability is called *augmented reality*.

Let's take it up another notch. Imagine a world where, instead of seeing a slightly modified version of your reality, you are transported to a beach. You can look around and see palm trees and jungles behind you.

Why stay earthbound? You are virtually transported to the space around Mars. As you look around, it is as if you are there on Mars.

Figure 12-21 looks like two images of the same planet. When your phone is inserted in the goggles, you get a 3-D image of the planet. You can also look around and navigate throughout the solar system. Trust me, this is a lot more convenient than space travel.

FIGURE 12-21:
A screen shot from VR Solar System from Onepixelsoft.

Why stay in the mainstream opinion of what is reality? Now we can all have an "Alice through the Looking Glass" experience. You can grow and shrink and see all kinds of unusual visions which are limited by your imagination.

There are some very, very cool demonstrations that leverage the capabilities of your phone. The Samsung offering comes at a great price compared to some of the other options out there. For that matter, you may have received the Samsung virtual reality goggles for free for preordering your phone.

There are additional VR applications and content in the Play Store. This is a rapidly changing area of the Play Store where new content is constantly being added. Be sure to check the Play Store regularly.

This should make your friends who own iPhone technology suitably jealous. What needs to happen is further application development to really take us to where this technology can go.

WARNING

Some of us unfortunately have the unpleasant experience of what is called virtual-reality sickness. This is similar, but not identical, to seasickness and car sickness. The most common symptoms are nausea and headaches. If this happens to you, some of the medicines that help seasickness may help you avoid this unpleasant sensation. Some say it also helps to be seated when using virtual reality. Plus, symptoms tend to diminish over time as your brain gets used to this experience. If the symptoms are too severe, virtual reality may just not be for you.

5
Getting Down to Business

IN THIS PART . . .

Download your calendars to your phone and upload new events to your electronic calendar.

Use Bixby to figure out what you're looking at.

Pay with Samsung Pay.

IN THIS CHAPTER

» Setting up events

» Downloading your calendars to your phone

» Uploading events to your PC

Chapter **13**

Using the Calendar

You might fall in love with your Galaxy S10 phone so much that you want to ask it out on a date. And speaking of dates, let's talk about your phone's calendar. The Galaxy S10 phone calendar functions are powerful, and they can make your life easier. With just a few taps, you can bring all your electronic calendars together to keep your life synchronized.

In this chapter, I show you how to set up the calendar that comes with your phone, which might be all you need. The odds are, though, that you have calendars elsewhere, such as on your work computer. So I also show you how to combine all your calendars with your Galaxy S10 phone. After you read this chapter, you'll have no excuse for missing a meeting. (Or, okay, a date.)

Some calendars use the term *appointments* for *events*. They are the same idea. I use the term *events*.

TIP

Syncing Calendars

Most likely, you already have at least two electronic calendars scattered in different places: A calendar tied to your work computer and a personal calendar. Now you have a third one — the one on your Samsung phone that is synced to your Gmail account.

Bringing together all your electronic calendars to one place, though, is one of the best things about your phone — as long as you're a faithful user of your electronic calendars, that is. To begin this process, you need to provide authorization to the respective places that your calendars are stored in the same way as you authorized access to your email accounts and contacts in Chapters 5 and 6. This authorization is necessary to respect your privacy.

If your phone doesn't have a Calendar icon on the Home screen, open the Calendar app from your App list. This same app works with the calendar that's stored on your phone and any digital calendars that you add.

When you first open this app, you see a calendar in monthly format, as shown in Figure 13-1. I discuss other calendar views in the next section.

Options link

FIGURE 13-1:
The monthly calendar display.

When you add an account to your phone, such as your personal or work email account, your Facebook account, or Dropbox, you're asked whether you want to sync your calendar. The default setting for syncing is typically every hour.

Unless you get a warning message that alerts you to a communications problem, your phone now has the latest information on appointments and meeting requests. Your phone continues to sync automatically. It does all this syncing in the background; you may not even notice that changes are going on.

WARNING

You could encounter scheduling conflicts if others can create events for you on your digital calendar. Be aware of this possibility. It can be annoying (or worse) to think you have free time, offer it, and then find that someone else took it.

Setting Calendar Display Preferences

Before you get too far into playing around with your calendar, you'll want to choose how you view it.

If you don't have a lot of events, using the month calendar shown in Figure 13-1 is probably a fine option. On the other hand, if your day is jam-packed with personal and professional events, the daily or weekly schedules might prove more practical. Switching views is easy. For example, just tap the three lines at the top of the calendar, which in this case displays Apr 2016, to bring up the options. These are shown in Figure 13-2.

If you tap Week, you see the weekly display, as shown in Figure 13-3.

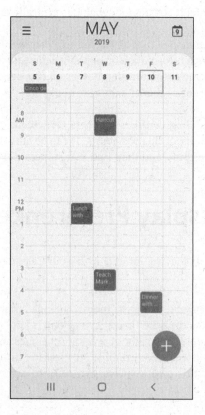

Year

Month ✓

Week

Day

Tasks

Reminder

FIGURE 13-2:
The Calendar
Display Options
pop-up menu.

MAY
2019

S	M	T	W	T	F	S
5	6	7	8	9	10	11

Cinco de

8 AM — Haircut

9

10

11

12 PM — Lunch with ...

1

2

3 — Teach Mark

4 — Dinner with ...

5

6

7

FIGURE 13-3:
The weekly
calendar display.

Or tap the Day button at the top of the calendar to show the daily display, as shown in Figure 13-4.

FIGURE 13-4:
The daily
calendar display.

To see what events you have upcoming, regardless of the day they're on, you might prefer List view. Tap the List button at the top of the calendar to see a list of your activities.

TIP

The weekly and daily calendars show only a portion of the day. You can slide the screen to see the time slots earlier and later. You can also pinch and stretch to seem more or less of the time slots.

There is also an annual calendar, as seen in Figure 13-5. This is so busy that it does not allow you to see any appointments. It is primarily useful for setting dates out in the future.

FIGURE 13-5:
The annual
calendar display.

Setting Other Display Options

In addition to the default display option, you can set other personal preferences for the calendar on your phone. To get to the settings for the calendar, tap the More link on the daily, weekly, or monthly calendars and tap Settings. Doing so brings up the screen shown in Figure 13-6.

Look and feel

First day of the week
Local default

Alternate calendar
None

Show week numbers

Show weather forecast
Show the weekly weather forecast on your calendar.

Hide declined events

Highlight specific time events
Show color highlights for events that last less than a day in month view.

More settings

Notifications

Alert settings

Lock time zone
Lock event times and dates to your selected time zone. They won't change if you move to another time zone.

FIGURE 13-6:
The Settings
options for the
calendar
application.

You have the following options:

>> **First day of week:** The standard in the United States is that a week is displayed from Sunday to Saturday. If you prefer the week to start on Saturday or Monday, you can change it here.

>> **Alternate Calendars:** The default is the Gregorian Calendar. However, if you're among the more than one billion people who use the Chinese lunar calendar, you're in luck! Tap this option and you'll see the Chinese lunar date on the calendar. The same applies for the Korean lunar calendar, the Vietnamese lunar calendar, and some others.

>> **Show week numbers:** Some people prefer to see the week number on the weekly calendar. If you count yourself among those, check this option.

>> **Show weather forecast:** If you look at the monthly calendar shown in Figure 13-1, you can see an image on some of the days representing the weather forecast. If you like seeing this, you can keep this information. If you feel like it takes up too much real estate on your screen, you can delete it.

>> **Hide declined events:** When some of us decline an event, we don't care to hear about it again. Others may want to keep a reminder of the declined event in case the situation changes (or in case nothing better comes along). The default setting is to hide declined events; if you want to see them, deselect this box.

>> **Highlight specific time events:** Selecting this option shows color for events that last less than a day, but only when you're in the Month calendar.

>> **Notification:** When an event is approaching, you can have the phone alert you with a pop-up, signal a notification on the status line, or do nothing. The default is to give you a notification, but you can change that option here.

>> **Alert Settings:** It helps some of us to be reminded about an appointment a few minutes before we are to be somewhere. Others of us find this annoying. This setting lets you choose whether you get a reminder or not and how far in advance you will be reminded.

>> **Lock time zone:** When you travel to a new time zone, your phone will take on the new time zone. Under most circumstances, this is a nice convenience. However, it may be confusing to some. If you prefer that the calendar remain in your home time zone, check this option.

Creating an Event on the Right Calendar

An important step in using a calendar when mobile is creating an event. It's even more important to make sure that the event ends up on the right calendar. This section covers the steps to make this happen.

Creating, editing, and deleting an event

Here's how to create an event — referred to as (well, yeah) an "event" — on your phone. Start from one of the calendar displays shown in Figures 13-1, 13-3, or 13-4. Tap the bright green circle with the plus (+) sign at the bottom right of the calendar. Doing so brings up the pop-up screen shown in Figure 13-7 (without the keyboard).

Title		●
Start	Mon, Apr 1	8:00 AM
End	Mon, Apr 1	9:00 AM

Time All day

✉ • galaxysfordummies@gmail.com

🔔 10 mins before   Add

🗁 **Repeat**
Never

◎ Location

▤ Notes

⚇ Invitee

🌐 **Time zone**
(GMT-08:00) Pacific Standard Time

Cancel   Save

||| ○   ‹

FIGURE 13-7:
The Create Event
screen.

The only required information to get things started is a memorable event name and the Start and End times.

You need the following information at hand when making an event:

>> **Calendar:** Decide on which calendar you want to keep this event. Figure 13-7 shows that this event will be stored on the Gmail calendar. This is indicated by showing my Gmail account next to the blue dot in the middle of the screen. When you tap this selection, the phone presents you with the other calendars you've synced to your phone; you can store an event on any of them.

>> **Title:** Call the event something descriptive so that you can remember what it is without having to open it up.

>> **Start and End:** The two entry fields for the start and end times. Select the All Day toggle if the event is a full-day event.

>> **Notification:** This field lets you set how soon before an event your phone will alert you that you have an upcoming event. This makes it less likely that you'll be late to an appointment if you set this alert to accommodate your travel time.

>> **Location:** This setting ties in to the Google Maps app, allowing you to enter an address or a landmark. You can also just enter text.

If you want, you can enter more details on the meeting by adding the following:

>> **Repeat:** This option is useful for recurring events, such as weekly meetings.

>> **Invitees:** This allows you to have a group meeting by entering multiple contacts.

>> **Notes:** Add information that you find useful about that meeting.

>> **Privacy:** This is the same idea as the Show Me As option, but for non-Outlook-based calendars.

>> **Time zone:** If you and everyone that is invited will be in the same time zone, you are set. If you happen to be in another time zone or some of the invitees are in other time zones, you can use this option to ensure that you are not setting a meeting off business hours, or worse, in the middle of the night.

After you fill in the obligatory (and any optional) fields and settings, tap the Save link at the bottom of the page. The event is stored in whichever calendar you selected when you sync.

After you save an event, you can edit it, share it, or delete it by tapping it on any of your calendars. It appears as shown in Figure 13-8. Now you can

>> **Edit:** This brings up the information as entered. Make your changes and tap Save.

>> **Share:** You can send this event as an attachment to anyone as a text.

>> **Delete:** To delete an event, you simply tap the garbage can icon at the bottom of the screen and the event is gone.

<

Irving in Irvine   ●

| Start | Mon, Apr 1 | 8:00 AM |
| End | Mon, Apr 1 | 9:00 AM |

Time   All day

⊡ • galaxysfordummies@gmail.com

🔔 10 mins before   Add

∨ View more

<   Share   🗑 Delete

||| O   <

FIGURE 13-8:
The Edit Event
screen.

TIP

You can also create an event by tapping the calendar itself twice. Tapping it twice brings up a pop-up (refer to Figure 13-7) where you can enter the event details.

Keeping events separate and private

When you have multiple calendars stored in one place (in this case, your phone), you might get confused when you want to add a new event. It can be even more confusing when you need to add the real event on one calendar and a placeholder on another.

Suppose your boss is a jerk and to retain your sanity, you need to find a new job. You send your resume to the arch-rival firm, Plan B, which has offices across town. Plan B is interested and wants to interview you at 3 p.m. next Tuesday. All good news.

The problem is that your current boss demands that you track your every move on the company calendaring system. His draconian management style is to berate people if they're not at their desks doing work when they're not at a scheduled meeting. (By the way, I am not making up this scenario.)

You follow my drift. You don't want Snidely Whiplash trudging through your calendar, sniffing out your plans to exit stage left, and making life more miserable if Plan B doesn't work out. Instead, you want to put a reasonable-sounding placeholder on your work calendar, while putting the real event on your personal calendar. You can easily do this from your calendar on your Samsung Galaxy S10. When you're making the event, you simply tell the phone where you want the event stored, making sure to keep each event exactly where it belongs.

The process begins with the Create Event screen. You bring this up by tapping the + sign in the green circle seen at the bottom-right corner of any of the calendars seen in Figures 13-1, 13-3, or 13-4. The information for the real event is shown on the left in Figure 13-9. The fake event is shown on the right. This is the one that is saved to your work email. The colored dot by the work address helps you be aware that this is a different calendar.

Real Appointment on Phone	Fake Appointment on Work E-mail
Interview with Plan B ●	Doctor's appointment ●
Start Fri, Apr 26 3:00 PM	Start Fri, Apr 26 3:00 PM
End Fri, Apr 26 4:00 PM	End Fri, Apr 26 4:00 PM
(Time | All day)	(Time | All day)
✉ • galaxysfordummies@gmail.com	✉ • ahardworker@badcompany.com

FIGURE 13-9: The Add an Event screen on your phone.

Now, when you look at your calendar on your phone, you see two events at the same time. (Check it out in Figure 13-10.) The Galaxy S10 doesn't mind if you make two simultaneous events.

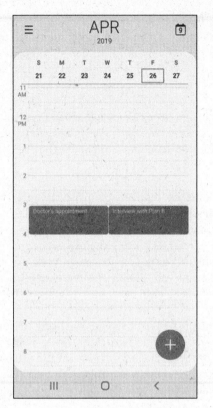

FIGURE 13-10:
Two events on
the same day on
your phone
calendar.

Under the circumstances, this is what you wanted to create. As long as your boss doesn't see your phone, you're safe — to try to find more fulfilling employment, that is.

Chapter **14**

Talking with Bixby

B ixby is Samsung's intelligent agent (IA). The purpose of an intelligent agent is to anticipate your questions and get information faster than tapping or typing. It typically involves simply speaking to your phone and having it do what you're asking without having to tap or type.

This IA thing can be confusing, so let me break it down for you. There are three main capabilities where Bixby comes in handy:

» Bixby Home summarizes the latest news from many of your most important apps.

» Bixby Vision can tell you what you're looking at. This includes telling what the price is, what the barcode means, how many calories are in the food, whether the fancy wine label really contain good wine, or how wonderful you would look with Sephora eyeshadow.

» Bixby Voice app can recognize your voice, take care of many phone commands, and respond back to you.

The deal with Bixby is that you can take or leave whatever features are there. If you like tapping and typing, Bixby understands. The intent of Bixby is to take the new functions of your smartphone and make it that much easier. If it's more than you can accept, that's okay. On the other hand, this is pretty exciting!

How happy you are with this app depends on how accurate Bixby is at doing what you want. In some ways, Bixby is spot on. In other cases, you may question why Samsung released this product. If you're disappointed with Bixby, my best advice is to try again at some point in the future. Bixby is continuously working to improve itself. In fact, you may be asked for permission to update Bixby Labs. This is the way you help Samsung improve Bixby, which in turn makes the app more accurate.

To help you with your next steps regarding Bixby, first I explore Bixby Home and how to access it. Then I cover Bixby Vision and Bixby Voice.

Bringing Up Bixby

Bixby Home is all about getting you summaries of the information you want to see the most in the most efficient way for you. Bixby Home gives you summaries of information from a variety of different apps. Each summary is called a *Bixby card.*

The simplest way to get to Bixby Home, shown in Figure 14-1, is to swipe to the right from your phone's home page. I talk more about voice interaction with Bixby later in this chapter.

Bixby Home is made up of "cards" that relate to popular applications you have on your phone. The cards give you a quick highlight of what's up. You can have as many or as few cards as you want on Bixby Home. You can see all the options for setting up cards by tapping the Bixby Options icon, shown in the upper-right corner of Figure 14-1. This brings up a list of Bixby options (see Figure 14-2).

When you tap Cards, you can see all the applications that you could potentially set up as cards on your Bixby page (see Figure 14-3).

When you tap Apps under Home Cards, you see the apps you've already down-loaded, as well as apps that you may want to download. This list will continue to change as more apps support the Bixby card. If you see an app is supported, but you haven't downloaded it yet, simply tap the Download button, and you'll be taken to the page within the Google Play Store so you can add it immediately.

If you want to delete a card, you simply slide the card to the right. Figure 14-4 shows Bixby Home after you've swiped to the right.

You have some flexibility in the placement of the cards. Each card has two horizontal lines in the upper-right corner.

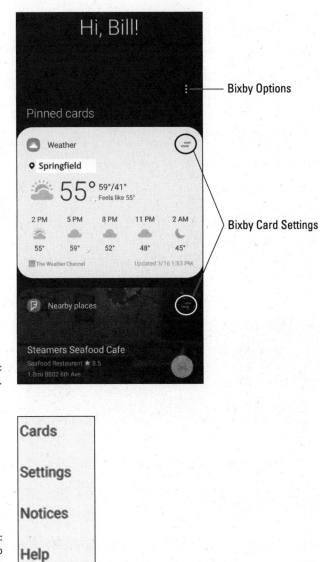

Hi, Bill!

Bixby Options

Pinned cards

Weather

Springfield

55° 59°/41°
Feels like 55°

2 PM	5 PM	8 PM	11 PM	2 AM
55°	59°	52°	48°	45°

The Weather Channel   Updated 3/16 1:53 PM

Bixby Card Settings

Nearby places

Steamers Seafood Cafe
Seafood Restaurant ★ 8.5
1.8mi 8802 6th Ave

FIGURE 14-1:
Bixby Home.

Cards

Settings

Notices

Help

FIGURE 14-2:
The Bixby pop-up
menu page.

If you're particularly interested in one card, you can tap Pin to Top. This will move that card to the top of the list. You can also ask it to refresh itself. That will cause it to check if there is new information.

The Bixby page is very handy when you're actively using your phone. It makes whatever you consider to be most important readily available with two quick presses of a button or a quick swipe to the right from the Home page.

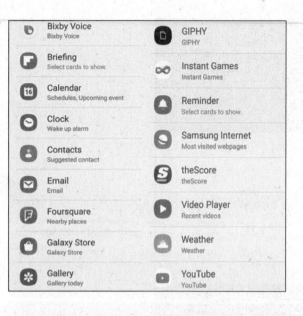

FIGURE 14-3:
The Bixby Card
options.

FIGURE 14-4:
Getting rid of an
active Bixby card.

Visualizing What You Can Do with Bixby Vision

In Chapter 9, I point out the Bixby Vision option in the viewfinder. When you have the camera app open, you can tap the link to launch Bixby Vision. Bixby Vision can then tell you information about what the camera is pointed at:

>> If it's an object, Bixby Vision can tell you what the object is and how much you can buy it for online.

>> If it's a barcode or QR code, Bixby Vision can tell you what the code means.

>> If it's text, Bixby Vision can read it and convert it to text. You can then translate that text into any of 108 languages.

» If it's a landmark, Bixby Vision can tell you where it's located.

» If it's a wine label, Bixby Vision can tell you the ranking of the wine and what food pairs well with it.

How Bixby Vision works is simple. You open the camera application and point the camera so that it has a good view of the object, document, barcode, text, or wine label just as described back in Chapter 9 (see Figure 14-5).

Normal camera viewfinder   Camera viewfinder with Bixby Vision

FIGURE 14-5:
A typical image
from the
Viewfinder before
and after tapping
Bixby Vision.

When you tap the Bixby icon on the viewfinder, your phone starts trying to figure out what it is and what you want. In Figure 14-5, it sees an apple and then asks you whether you want it to search this object as an image to find out what it is or whether you're interested in shopping for this item or some other thing it can do.

Let's say that I want to buy an apple. I tap the Shopping icon. The results are in Figure 14-6.

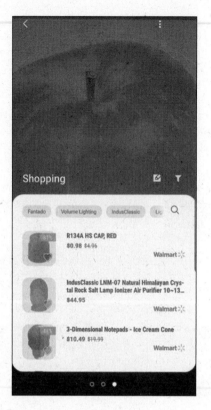

FIGURE 14-6:
Shopping options
presented based
on Figure 14-5.

So, I really wanted to get prices on fresh honey crisp apples from the state of Washington. The top choice was a red cap. The second choice is a red salt lamp/air purifier (pay attention, Bixby Labs!).

The point is that Bixby Vision does its best to interpret what you want. It does better on some things, like UPC product codes. If you show it text, it will start copying it.

Bixby will present one or more of these icons based on what it thinks is in the image and what you want. Not only is this fun, but you might save some money when you're shopping!

Blabbing with Bixby

Every science-fiction movie worth its salt predicts a world where we speak to computers rather than typing in data. Normal conversation is about 150 words per minute, whereas even an expert typist can only type at 90 words per minute.

More important, talking is the most basic form of communication. The reality is that there are many technical obstacles to having voice recognition match the ideal of a computer perfectly interpreting the meaning of any user's verbal instructions.

That does not stop us from having some fun in the meantime. When Bixby includes Voice, you'll be able to make a phone call, send an email or a text, search the web, or even update your Facebook status and calendar with voice commands.

One of the quirks about Bixby is that Bixby Home, Bixby Vision, and Bixby Voice are each independent applications. Each has its own look and feel. Ultimately, it isn't a big deal because you use them for very different things. Just keep this in mind when you're setting up Bixby Voice. You'll probably use Bixby Voice most frequently, so when setting up your preferences, I encourage you to spend the most time getting it the way you like it. Ultimately, you may love this capability. Or you may find it to be a gimmick and not very useful. Either way, you can have some fun with it and, hopefully, it'll grow on you.

Look Ma! No Hands!

Say you want to call someone. In the old days, high-end mobile phones would require you to train the voice-recognition software to understand the basics of how you speak. No more. Just tell it who you want to call, by pressing and holding the Bixby button on the left side of your phone and saying, "Call Bill."

Be ready. In just a moment, it calls Bill. It's that easy.

However, if you know several people named Bill, your phone asks you (in a semi-pleasant voice) which "Bill" you want to call. You may have heard of "Siri" on the iPhone. Siri responds to questions you ask it. The Bixby app is the same idea, except it responds to the name "Bixby." After you teach Bixby your voice with a few basic commands, all you have to do is say, "Hi, Bixby."

If you want to call Bill Boyce, a person from your contact list, say "Hi, Bixby. Call Bill Boyce." Within a moment, his phone rings.

I get to the list of things that work with Bixby soon. For now, try a few of its simple-yet-valuable capabilities.

Setting Up Bixby for Your Voice

From the Bixby Settings page (refer to Figure 14-3), scroll down to Voice Wake-up and toggle the button to on. The screen shown in Figure 14-7 appears. When you're ready, tap the Bixby logo.

Preparing to learn your voice   Learning your voice

FIGURE 14-7:
The text
prepared by
Bixby,
ready to go.

You'll be asked to say "Hello, Bixby" a few times, as well as a few other phases. Then it's ready to go. You simply say, "Hi, Bixby" followed by your request.

Dictating a Text

To send a text, say the words, "Hi, Bixby. Send a text." Done. The text screen pops up.

Bixby asks you, "Who would you like to message?" Give the name. It looks up their number from your contact list. I say, "Ludwig van Beethoven." Bixby then asks you for your message. Go ahead and say what you would have typed.

Bixby then converts your words into a message. It displays what it thinks you said in a box, as shown in Figure 14-8.

Would you like me to send this message?

Messages

Recipients
Ludwig van Beethoven

Message
I'll be Bach

Send   Cancel

FIGURE 14-8:
The text prepared by Bixby, ready to go.

Read it before you send it. If it is correct, just say "Send" and off it goes. If it's incorrect, you can say "Cancel," and it won't send that message. You can then try again. It's that easy. Give it a try!

Preparing to Work with Bixby

Texting is a straightforward example, but it is just one of the tasks Bixby can do for you. You can ask Bixby to do all kinds of things on your phone. Some examples include

>> Telling you the time

>> Setting an alarm

>> Turning Wi-Fi on or off

- » Telling you the weather forecast
- » Setting a countdown timer
- » Recording your voice
- » Opening an app
- » Playing a playlist
- » Adding an appointment to your schedule
- » Finding a local restaurant, store, or public location
- » Navigating to an address or location

All you need to do is ask, and Bixby does a good job finding what you want. Here is the best way to learn what Bixby can do: Ask Bixby, "What services do you offer?" The screen shown in Figure 14-9 appears.

Here are some services available for you.

1-800-Flowers.com
Send birthday flowers

Accessibility
Turn on all Flash Notifications

Alarm and Timer
Set my Work alarm for 8 AM tomorrow

AR Emoji
Create AR Emoji

FIGURE 14-9: Bixby when you ask which services are available.

Each app comes with a suggestion under the app name. For example, the app suggests what you can do, such as "Send birthday flowers." You can learn more when you tap the 1-800-Flowers.com link. A complete list of apps is shown in Figure 14-10. This list is impressive.

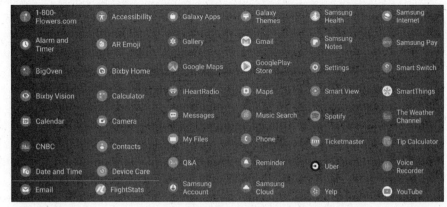

FIGURE 14-10:
List of Bixby services available to use with Bixby Voice.

Most applications have a pretty good list of commands. Figure 14-11 shows a more modest list of options for the Calculator app, to give you a sense of what's there.

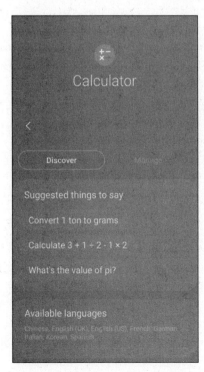

FIGURE 14-11:
Bixby commands for the Calculator app.

Go ahead and try some math problems to get the hang of it. Who knew math would be so easy? (And to think Mr. McCrea said that we wouldn't always have a calculator when we needed it.)

All this talking and calculating has made me a little hungry, but not too hungry that I can't ask Bixby, "Hi, Bixby. Where is the closest McDonald's using Google Maps?" Bixby comes back with some options, as shown in Figure 14-12.

FIGURE 14-12:
Bixby options on a location.

Then you can ask it for directions to the McDonald's you choose. This request causes Bixby to hand you over to your preferred navigation application, bringing up a screen like the one shown in Figure 14-13.

You could also use other apps, such as Yelp, if you prefer getting information other than just location. For example, if you want to find the best Italian restaurant in Seattle, just ask and you see Figure 14-14.

Now all you need to do is drive there safely and enjoy!

FIGURE 14-13:
Navigating to
the location
you requested.

FIGURE 14-14:
Asking for the
best restaurant
in the area.

Chapter **15**

Paying with Samsung Pay

S omeday in the future, you will be able to leave your wallet at home and just use your smartphone for all the stuff that you carry with you today. We are not there yet, but Samsung has implemented some technology that moves us toward that day.

You may reasonably ask why not carrying your wallet is such a big deal. Fair enough. The two main reasons are that it is more convenient and more secure. Samsung Pay takes us a long way to this ultimate goal. The reality is you will need to continue to carry your wallet with credit cards and cash for now.

For now, you'll need to decide for yourself whether the convenience that Samsung Pay does offer is worth the effort associated with setting it up. Samsung has gone to great lengths to make transactions more secure than simply using a credit card. Like so many of these things, the security is only as good as how the individual implements it.

With that awareness, some things about Samsung Pay are exceptionally cool. If you like to show off new technology to people, this is a good opportunity. In particular, you can one-up your smug friends who use Apple Pay with their iPhones. That capability alone is worth the price of admission for some of us.

How Mobile Payment Works

It helps to explain how mobile payments work to see how Samsung Pay helps you. The idea is that you walk up to the checkout stand at a retailer. You swipe your fingerprint on the reader, place your phone near the card reader, and instantly your transaction is done. The receipt prints, and you take your purchase and go on your merry way. The charge shows up on your credit card.

Besides a fingerprint, you can enter a four-digit PIN or a quick retinal scan by glancing at your phone. You choose the security option that is most convenient for you, and Samsung makes sure that everything flows securely. All the authorizations were set up when you set up the credit card with Samsung Pay.

Really. That's all there is.

It sounds so simple. The interesting thing is that this capability has been around in one form or another for over 20 years. Back in 1997, Mobil gas stations implemented contactless payment with their Speedpass. Users on the system would tap their Speedpass fobs that they would keep on the key ring on the reader installed on the gas pump.

Their credit card would be charged for the gas they pumped. Initially, the tap was all that it took to pay for the gas. Later, users needed to add their ZIP code to enhance security. In spite of Mobil's best efforts, the system had only moderate success. There are a range of reasons, but a major concern was that people were already hesitant to even carry yet another thing. It is the inclusion of some new technology within smartphones that makes it so much more convenient.

Visa and MasterCard also tried contactless systems with limited success. One of their major challenges is that not enough credit card readers support the contactless payment system. After years of trying, fewer than 10 percent of all credit card readers as recently as 2015 have this capability. Those readers that do support contactless payment have the logo shown in Figure 15-1.

FIGURE 15-1:
The contactless payment logo.

The contactless payment approach got a significant boost when Apple introduced the Apple Pay system on the iPhone in 2014. Like some other technologies that have struggled to find widespread acceptance, the implementation by Apple produced enough momentum to overcome resistance to its widespread use.

Examples include the Apple Macintosh with its use of a mouse, the Apple iPod revolutionizing the acceptance of MP3 players, and the Apple iPad creating a revolutionizing a trend for tablets. All of these technologies were pioneered by other companies before Apple made them popular.

The Apple Pay system has seen significant success in an area where others have struggled. The retailers with the contactless credit card technology have seen a huge increase in its use from iPhone customers.

With Samsung Pay, however, Samsung has leapfrogged Apple. Samsung Pay works similarly to Apple Pay with contactless payment devices. It also works with the vast majority of standard credit card readers. Take that, Apple!

While 10 percent of credit card readers in retailers today support contactless payment, another 85 percent of credit card readers at retailers have readers that can read the magnetic stripe on the back of your credit card. Samsung Pay along with your Galaxy S10 have the electronics built in to work with the contactless system but also the electronics to convince the magnetic stripe readers that you have swiped your card!

The technology within your phone that works with the standard credit card readers is called *Magnetic Secure Transmission,* or MST. When you place your phone near the magnetic stripe reader, it sends a very short range signal to the magnetic stripe reader on your card that simulates the signals it gets when you physically swipe a magnetic stripe reader.

Your imagination could go wild and come up with ways that fiendish people could potentially steal this technology. One can never say never, but there are extensive procedures that are put in place to set up this capability to prevent it in most instances. The rest of this chapter walks you through those processes.

Probably the biggest drawback in using this technology these days is that too few retail clerks know that it will work. They freak out the first time they see it as they are probably familiar with contactless payment methods, know that they do not have it, and do not know about this slick solution. They will want to ask you more about it, which will end up taking more time than if you were paying by writing a check and having to provide two forms of identification!

Getting Started with Samsung Pay

The first step in the process is to make sure that you have Samsung Pay on your Galaxy S10. As cool as this app is, there are many options to this technology, and your carrier may have preferred to not have it preloaded. No problem. Chapter 8 explains how to download applications from the Play Store. The Samsung Pay logo is seen in Figure 15-2.

It is easy to confuse Samsung Pay and Google Pay. These are two different applications. Google Pay is nice, but it does not have the Magnetic Secure Transmission capability that allows you to use mobile payments at many more retailers.

TIP

The app page description is shown in Figure 15-3. When you tap Install, you get the image on the right.

FIGURE 15-3:
The Samsung Pay app Play Store images before and after installation.

The Samsung Pay app works a little different than most other apps. The first time you open Samsung Pay, you will be given information on how to use it and be asked to put in your credit card information (in a very convenient way, by the way) and asked all kinds of permissions and agreements.

Once you have given all this information, Samsung Pay waits patiently at the bottom of your home pages, ready to meet your payment needs with nothing more than a quick swipe from the bottom of the screen. Most people would simply not use this app if they had to go digging through their screens to find the app. This way, you do not have to search to find the app and wait for it to come up.

Figure 15-4 shows the Home screen with the Samsung Pay launch button sitting at the bottom ready to appear with a quick flick.

FIGURE 15-4:
The Samsung Pay quick launch button.

Samsung Pay
Quick Launch
button

The launch button is also there on the Lock screen, so you don't even need to unlock your phone because you'll be using the exact same security steps before you can use your credit card.

Setting Up Samsung Pay

When you open the Samsung Pay app, you're greeted with a series of pages before you get to the Home screen seen in Figure 15-5. These pages include marketing introductions (which you don't need because you read this chapter), permissions and agreements (which you should give if you want to move forward), and some pages that verify that Samsung Pay can work on your phone.

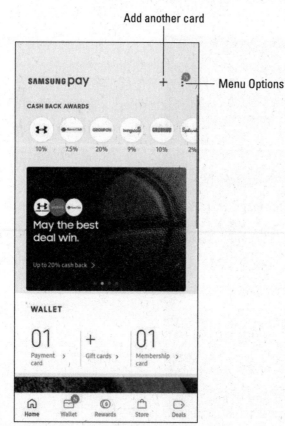

Add another card

Menu Options

FIGURE 15-5:
The Samsung Pay
Home Page.

The app wants to make sure that your phone has the right parts (your Galaxy S10 does, but that is not the case for every Android phone) and that you are in one of the 24 countries where Samsung Pay is accepted. You're set if you're in the United States, Canada, Puerto Rico, or China. You're out of luck if you're in, say, Yemen. Being in these countries is important for this app because each country has its own set of laws for payments, and Samsung may not have all the arrangements in place if you are not in one of these countries. New countries will be added as quickly as possible.

Read the agreements. In all likelihood, they are the same kind of agreements that exist in the fine print in your existing credit card and every time you sign your name to a credit card charge slip that affirms you won't pull any shenanigans. That said, I am your humble author, not your legal advisor, and you should feel comfortable with these agreements.

The next part of the initial setup process is to step through how you want to set up security. You have two security options when you are making a transaction: using your fingerprint or entering a PIN.

There are a few scenarios where using a Samsung Pay PIN rather than a fingerprint might make sense. In most cases, using your fingerprint is exceptionally convenient. Chapter 17 describes the process for using these biometric options as a security method. If you've already set these up in your phone, you see Figure 15-6. If you haven't set these up yet, the Samsung Pay application will walk you through the steps to do so. It's quick and easy.

FIGURE 15-6:
The Samsung
Pay credit card
Add page.

The next step is to enter your credit card information. When you tap the link that says Add Payment Card, you will be taken to a screen that lets you take an image of your credit card. This is seen in Figure 15-7. The left image is when the screen first comes up and the right image is when you have the desired credit card in the viewfinder.

Before taking an image of your card   After taking an image of your card

Viewfinder

FIGURE 15-7:
The Samsung Pay
credit card image
processing
screen.

The app then interprets the information on the front of your credit card and populates as many screens as possible with your credit card information. It will ask you to fill out the form seen in Figure 15-8 if it can't figure out the information on your card or the information is on the reverse side of the card.

TIP

Not every company that offers credit cards is signed up with Samsung Pay. You can check the Samsung website or tap the link in Figure 15-8 to check before you proceed. Otherwise, just go ahead and see whether things go through.

Tap Next, and Samsung Pay will seek to confirm things with your credit card company. This does not cost you anything. It just wants to make sure that when you do make a charge, everything will flow smoothly. One of the things the company will want to verify is that you are authorized to use that credit card. This means that either you need to be the primary cardholder or you need to coordinate with that person.

TIP

Keep in mind that scanning your fingerprint and tapping your phone on a credit card reader has the same legal implications as actually signing a credit slip.

When the credit card company verifies that everything is on the up and up, you get an acknowledgement like the one shown in Figure 15-9.

FIGURE 15-8:
The Populated
credit card data
fields.

FIGURE 15-9:
Card added
verification
screen.

Using Samsung Pay

First, pick something to buy at a store. Have a clerk ring it up and tell him you will pay with a credit card. Swipe the screen upward. You see the screen seen in Figure 15-10.

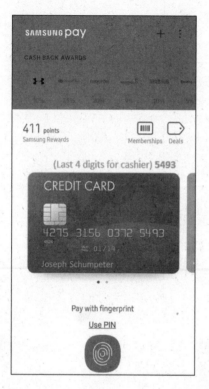

Enter your fingerprint by pressing the icon and you see a screen similar to Figure 15-11.

As seen in Figure 15-11, you should either hold your phone against where the credit card reader would read the magnetic stripe or where there is the contactless payment system logo if it is available.

The semicircle above your signature will start counting down, and your phone will vibrate to let you know that it is transmitting. You will hear a beep if it all goes through. If it fails for some reason, you can try again simply by reentering your security option.

Place the back of the device
against the card/NFC reader.

FIGURE 15-11:
Samsung Pay
payment screen
after reading
fingerprint.

TIP

This process works with the vast majority of credit card readers. This does not work well, however, with credit card readers where you insert your card into the machine and pull it out quickly. This type of reader is mostly used on gasoline pumps. Sorry.

Managing Samsung Pay

As long as you pay your credit card bills and keep your credit card account at the bank, this app is relatively self-sufficient. Still, you will need to access the app settings from time to time. You get there by tapping the Samsung Pay logo on the app screen. This will bring up the screen shown in Figure 15-5.

To add a new credit or debit card, tap the Add link and go through the process described in the section "Setting Up Samsung Pay," earlier in this chapter.

Adding a second card is easy, and the images will stack up when above each other on this page. The quick launch link brings up whatever card is on the top. If you want to change to use a different credit card, you can flip through the options.

You tap the three dots to get a pop-up for the settings of Samsung Pay and select Settings. The settings page is shown in Figure 15-12.

SETTINGS

FAVORITE CARDS

Use Favorite Cards
Lock screen, Home screen, Screen off

Manage Favorite Cards

VERIFICATION METHOD

Fingerprint

Change Samsung Pay PIN

GENERAL

Notifications
Receive notifications

Marketing information
Receive marketing notifications and
emails from Samsung Pay, Samsung, and
Samsung partners.

Fast checkout

FIGURE 15-12:
Samsung Pay
settings screen.

Profile

If you want to change the settings for or delete a credit card, all you have to do is tap on the Manager Favorite Cards link. All the information associated with that card will appear in the screen.

Enjoy your spending!

6

The Part of Tens

Get the most out of your phone.

Protect yourself if you lose your phone.

Discover what features will be coming in future versions.

Chapter **16**

Ten Ways to Make Your Phone Totally Yours

A smartphone is a very personal device. From the moment you take it out of the box and strip off the packaging, you begin to make it yours. By the end of the first day, even though millions of your type of phone may have been sold, there's no other phone just like yours.

This is the case because of the phone calls you make and because of all the options you can set on the phone and all the information you can share over the web. Your contacts, music files, downloaded videos, texts, and favorites make your phone a unique representation of who you are and what's important to you.

Even with all this "you" on your phone, this chapter covers ten or so ways to further customize your phone beyond what this book covers. Some of these suggestions involve accessories. Others involve settings and configurations. All are worth considering.

When it comes to accessories, your carrier's retail store has many good options. And oodles, heaps, loads, and tons of options for your phone are available outside the carrier's retail store. There is no need to limit yourself.

Using a Bluetooth Speaker

In just a matter of a couple of years, Bluetooth speakers have gone from an interesting (and expensive) option to mainstream. Prices have come down quickly, and the variety of designs for the speakers has grown dramatically. In all cases, you get the benefit of being able to play your music on your phone without the inconvenience of having headphones. You also get a speakerphone, although the quality of the audio can vary dramatically from Bluetooth speaker to Bluetooth speaker.

This accessory is best purchased in a brick-and-mortar store where you can listen to a variety of choices. Although syncing with a number of speaker choices can be tedious, it's the only way you'll know if a particular Bluetooth speaker meets your needs.

Although sound quality is essential, the folks in the industrial-design department have been having a lot of fun coming up with ways for the Bluetooth speaker to look. Figure 16-1 shows a range of options for the most popular form factors.

Rectangular form factor   Sound Bar form factor   Can form factor

FIGURE 16-1:
Popular Bluetooth speaker form factors.

The most popular options are basically a rectangle, the can style, and the sound bar. Each company has its own twist, but these options represent what you can see in the high-volume stores.

Fortunately, you live in a world where designers can get creative. Figure 16-2 shows some of the more exceptional designs.

House of Marley   CRAZY BABY levitating speaker   SPI-Home Pelican speaker

FIGURE 16-2:
Unusual designs for Bluetooth speakers.

The House of Marley, for example, uses unconventional design and recycled material to stand out in the market. CRAZY BABY makes the Mars series, which includes a levitating speaker. SPI Home produces a Bluetooth speaker built into a variety of garden statues, including a pelican.

There is no shortage of imagination when it comes to Bluetooth. Be sure to consider all your options. Before you settle on the mainstream options at the local mall, do some research off the beaten path. You'll be amazed at the range of options.

Cruising in the Car

You may have gotten the idea that I am concerned about your safety when you're using your phone. True, but I'm also concerned with *my* safety when you're using your phone. I would like you to have a Bluetooth speaker in your car when driving in my neighborhood, if you please.

Many new cars have a built-in Bluetooth system within the car stereo that connects to a microphone somewhere on the dash as well as to your car speakers. It's smart enough to sense an incoming call and mutes your music in response.

If you don't have such a setup, there are lots of good options for car speakers. Figure 16-3 shows an example.

FIGURE 16-3: Bluetooth car speaker.

A closely related accessory is a car mount. A *car mount* will hold your phone in a place you can easily observe as you drive. The mount attaches to an air vent, the dashboard, or the windshield.

You could always put your phone on the seat next to you, but that's for amateurs. Instead, offer your phone a place of honor with a car docking station. It makes accessing your phone while you drive safer and easier. Some see getting a car mount as a luxury, but my view is that if you need to upgrade your navigation software, you need a vehicle mount.

WARNING

Be sure to put away the docking station when you park. Even an empty docking station is a lure for a thief.

Figure 16-4 shows a typical vehicle mount. There are a great variety of options. Some mounts grip the phone, while other involve magnets. Some mounts use suction cups to hold onto the inside of your windshield, some clip on air vents, and still others you can screw into your dashboard. Many allow you to plug in a car charger, while others offer wireless charging. They cost $30 to $50. You can get these at your carrier's store, at Best Buy, or at Amazon.

FIGURE 16-4:
A standard vehicle mount.

More economical vehicle mounts are available that do not include a wireless charging pad. Figure 16-5 shows an example from SlipGrip that costs closer to $30.

This version is special because it is specifically designed to work with larger protective cases. It can be a hassle to have to remove the protective case from your phone to insert it in a vehicle mount. In addition to a car mount, SlipGrip also offers a mount for your bicycle.

TIP

When shopping for a car mount or a bike mount, be sure to consider the extra girth associated with a case. If you don't use a case (which is a mistake), you just need to be sure that the mount is compatible with a Galaxy S10. If you have a case on your phone (which is anything but a mistake), be sure the mount will work with the Galaxy S10 *and* the case.

FIGURE 16-5:
A SlipGrip
vehicle mount.

Considering Wireless Charging Mats

Those industrial designers have certainly gone crazy with Bluetooth speakers. They have also been having a field day on wireless charging options.

Most wireless charging mats are designed with the idea that you can place your phone on the mat, and technology will do the rest. You can get a standard Samsung wireless charging pad, shown in Figure 16-6, for about $50. Samsung also offers the Fast Charging pad, which will charge your phone from stone-cold dead to 100 percent in just a few hours. This capability costs a little more, closer to $70.

FIGURE 16-6:
The Samsung
wireless charging
pad (left) and the
Samsung Fast
Charging pad
(right).

If these are too conventional for you, more options are out there as well. Figure 16-7 shows some of the more interesting options. You can go colorful, high-tech, or back to nature. Your choice.

Look for more options going forward!

TYLT Wireless Charging Stand

Native Union Eclipse Charger

FIGURE 16-7:
More exotic
wireless
charging pads.

Wood Charging Stand

Making a Statement with Wraps

Not the sandwich kind of wraps. I'm talking about the kind of wrap that lets you customize the non-glass portion of the S10.

The Samsung Galaxy S10 is very attractive, but you can spruce it up with an adhesive covering called a wrap from Skinit at www.skinit.com. These designs can express more of what is important to you. As a side benefit, they can protect your phone from minor scratches.

Figure 16-8 shows some design options for a skin. It comes with cut-outs for speakers, plugs, microphones, and cameras specifically for the Galaxy S10. Putting the skin on is similar to putting on a decal, although it has a little give in the material to make positioning easier. The skin material and adhesive are super high-tech and have enough give to allow klutzes like me (who struggle with placing regular decals) to fit the nooks and crannies of the phone like an expert.

If you're not crazy about Skinit's designs, you can make your own with images of your own choosing. Just be sure that you have the rights to use the images!

Galaxy S10 Skins

FIGURE 16-8: Some sample wrap designs.

White Marble   USA Flag   Van Gogh Starry Night   Tie Dye

You Look Wonderful: Custom Screen Images

In addition to the shortcuts on your extended Home screen, you can also customize the images that are behind the screen. You can change the background to one of three options:

» Choose a neutral background image (similar to the backgrounds on many PCs) from the Wallpaper Gallery. Figure 16-9 shows a selection of background images that are standard on your phone.

» Any picture from your Gallery can be virtually stretched across the seven screens of your home page. (Read more about the Gallery in Chapter 9.)

» Opt for a theme that changes the background and fonts.

The pictures from your Gallery and the Wallpaper Gallery are images that you can set by pressing and holding the Home screen. In a moment, you see icons appear. Select Wallpapers and pick the image you want. Many are free; others you can download for less than a dollar.

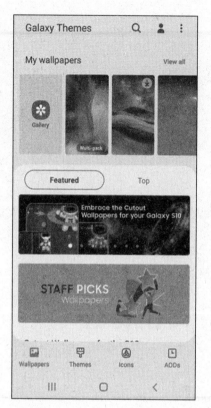

FIGURE 16-9:
Standard
wallpaper
sample images.

The themes take it to a different level. In addition to the background, the phone will change the fonts and many of the basic icons. You can select different themes, as shown in Figure 16-10, that follow different color and font combinations. There are lots of options.

A few samples also come on your phone. You may be a pink kind of person or a space nut. If these options aren't to your taste, tap the Store link at the top of the page to see a range of options. If you do not see one you like today, be sure to check back as developers are adding new themes all the time. Do yourself a favor, and see if any of these strike a chord with you.

FIGURE 16-10:
Different theme
options.

Empowering Power Savings

Imagine that you're flying on a short hop from Smallville to Littleton. You are about to take off when air traffic control tells the pilot that the plane needs to wait on the tarmac. Unfortunately, you are low on battery. The pilot says that it is okay to use your mobile phone.

Because you do not know how long this will take, you pull out your phone, go to Settings, and tap Battery. From here, you put it in Power Savings Mode. This slows down a lot of cool features. For example, it dims the screen, slows the processors and mobile data speeds, and kills the vibration mode. This extends the battery life with minor sacrifices to what you can do with your phone. The apps all run, but perhaps not as fast.

Then the pilot says that your plane has a flat tire, the maintenance crew went home, and you could be sitting there for hours.

This time you open Settings, tap Device Care, tap Battery, tap Power Mode, and put your phone in Maximum Power Savings mode. Your beautiful, powerful smartphone has instantly turned itself into a dumb feature phone. You won't be able to watch a full-length feature film. However, you now have enough battery to make and take phone calls and text messages for hours. This is not an exact science and your mileage may vary, but switching to this mode can multiply the time your smartphone can operate as a phone by eight to ten times. If you aren't ready to return to the 2000s, you can use the Medium power savings mode.

Controlling Your Home Electronics

Traditional home appliances are getting smarter, offering more capabilities for better performance. One problem they have is that adding rows of control buttons (so that you can control those new capabilities) complicates manufacture. So, the next generation of appliances has begun to add a small LCD screen to the appliance. This can look slick, but it costs a lot and is prone to breakage. Also, the fancy capabilities involve pushing a confusing combination of buttons with cryptic messages displayed on a tiny screen.

The latest idea is to omit the screen altogether and give you control of the settings through an application on your smartphone. Your appliance retains the very basic buttons but allows you to use the fancy capabilities by setting them through your phone. You just download the free application made by the manufacturer from the Google Play Store, and you have your beautiful and logical user interface to control your new product — no strings attached.

For example, your new oven will allow you to turn it on and set the temperature without using a smartphone. However, if you want it to start preheating at 5:30 p.m. so that you can put the casserole in right when you walk in the door, you can set that up through your phone.

Wearing Wearables

Wearables are a class of mobile accessories that have been getting a lot of attention. For the most part, wearables are connected via Bluetooth and typically worn as a watch, although you can wear some sensors in athletic shoes. Samsung offers its wearables under the brand name Samsung Watch Active (see Figure 16-11).

FIGURE 16-11:
Samsung Watch
Active wearables.

In addition to telling the time, these wearables give you notifications, weather, and texts and track some relevant information, such as the amount of exercise you've done. These images look like conventional, but stylish analog watches. It shows you texts, a phone dialing pad, your altitude, and the useful information that would otherwise be shown on your phone. How cool is that?!

Using Your Phone as a PC

Your phone has all the computing power of a PC. Wouldn't it be nice if you didn't have to carry a laptop? Enter the Samsung Dex (see Figure 16-12).

FIGURE 16-12:
Samsung
Dex Cable.

The Dex Docking Cable may look like a charging cable, but it's so much more. When you connect the little connector (USB-C) to your phone, you can connect the other end into a PC monitor or a TV. What's on your beautiful small screen now appears on your beautiful big screen! If you connect a Bluetooth keyboard and mouse, it will almost seem like you have a regular PC. This is much smaller and more convenient than lugging around even the lightest laptop.

Creating Your Own AR Emoji

I've saved the best for last: You can take a self-portrait and make your own emoji that becomes an integral part of your Galaxy S10. You may be used to sending smiley faces, frown faces, and winks. Now you can send *you*.

Let me show you what I mean. Let's say that you're President Teddy Roosevelt, and you're tired after a successful day of assaulting San Juan Hill, busting trusts, and rescuing orphan bear cubs. You sit down with your new Galaxy S10 smartphone, and decide to send a text to your pal Thomas Jefferson. (They were pals, right? They posed together for Mount Rushmore.) Instead of sending the conventional smiley face, you decide to send an AR Emoji. Figure 16-13 shows what you look like in real life and your smiling emoji.

When you create an emoji of yourself, this app creates a series of animations, called GIFs, that provide animation of your emoji showing a variety of emotions. These are stored in the Gallery app, and you can send them to anyone you like.

So, let's say you're happy because you just got word that they completed the Panama Canal. You send a happy emoji. You try, but fail, to institute a federal income tax, so you send a sad emoji. When you're campaigning in Milwaukee, saloonkeeper John Schrank shoots you in the chest, but you keep on talking another 90 minutes. When you're done speechifying, you're quite cross with Mr. Shrank, so you send him an angry emoji. These emojis are shown in Figure 16-14. The complete library from the Gallery app is shown in Figure 16-15.

Portrait of Teddy Roosevelt

Emoji of Teddy Roosevelt

FIGURE 16-13:
The real image
and the emoji
image.

Happy Emoji

Sad Emoji

Angry Emoji

FIGURE 16-14:
Emoji options.

If you find your emoji to not quite capture you, you do have the ability to modify the image. You can add or take away hair, as well as adjust the color and style. You can also add glasses (although for some reason they don't have the pince-nez glasses Teddy Roosevelt liked to wear). You can also change attire as needed.

FIGURE 16-15:
Emoji options
stored in your
Gallery app.

When you're an emoji in your phone, you and your phone are in it for the long haul!

» **Avoiding losing your phone in the first place**

» **Protecting yourself if you do lose your phone**

Chapter **17**

Ten (Or So) Ways to Make Your Phone Secure

B ack in the "old" days, it sure was frustrating to have your regular-feature phone lost or stolen. You would lose all your contacts, call history, and texts. Even if you backed up all your contacts, you would have to reenter them in your new phone. What a hassle.

WARNING

The good news is that your smartphone saves all your contacts on your email accounts. The bad news is that, unless you take some steps outlined in this chapter, evildoers could conceivably drain your bank account, get you fired, or even have you arrested.

Do I have your attention? Think of what would happen if someone were to get access to your PC at home or at work. He or she could wreak havoc on your life.

A malevolent prankster could send an email from your work email address under your name. It could be a rude note to the head of your company. It could give phony information about a supposedly imminent financial collapse of your company to the local newspaper. It could be a threat to the U.S. president, generating a visit from the Secret Service.

Here's the deal: If you have done anything with your smartphone as described in this book past Chapter 3, I expect you'll want to take steps to protect your smartphone. This is the burden of having a well-connected device. Fortunately, most of the steps are simple and straightforward.

Using a Good Case

The Samsung Galaxy S10 is sleek and beautiful. The Galaxy S10 has a really cool design that draws attention from people walking by. Plus, the front is made of Gorilla Glass from Corning. This stuff is super-durable and scratch-resistant.

So why am I telling you to cover this all up? It's like buying a fancy dress for a prom or wedding and wearing a coat all night. Yup. It's necessary for safe mobile computing.

WARNING

Speaking from personal experience, dropping a Galaxy phone on concrete can break the glass and scramble some of the innards. This can happen if you simply keep your phone in a pocket.

There are lots of choices for cases. The most popular are made of silicone, plastic, or leather. There are different styles that meet your needs from many manufacturers.

Samsung offers several good options, as shown in Figure 17-1.

LED Wallet Cover   Silicone Cover   Leather Cover

FIGURE 17-1:
Samsung cases for the Galaxy S10E, S10, and S10+.

Otterbox is a brand that has been marking cases for multiple levels of protection. The Defender Series for the Galaxy S10, its highest level of protection, is seen in black in Figure 17-2. You can get other levels of protection with more colors if you prefer.

Strada Series   Symmetry Series   Defender Series

FIGURE 17-2:
Otterbox cases
for the Samsung
Galaxy S10E, S10,
and S10+.

TIP

I am told by the cooler members of my clan that wearing the belt clip is the modern equivalent of wearing a pocket protector.

You don't just use a good case so that you can hand off a clean used phone to the next lucky owner. A case makes it a little less likely that you will lose your phone. Your Galaxy S10 in its naked form is shiny glass and metal, which are slippery. Cases tend to have a higher coefficient of friction and prevent your phone from slipping out of your pocket when you take a ride in an Uber car.

More significantly, a case protects your phone against damage. If your phone is damaged, you have to mail it or bring it to a repair shop. The problem is that many people who bring their phones in for repair don't wipe the personal information off their devices. You really hope that the repair shop can pop off the broken piece, pop on a new one, and send you on your way. It's rarely that easy. Typically, you need to leave your phone in the hands of strangers for some period of time. For the duration of the repair, said strangers have access to the information on your phone.

The good news is that most workers who repair phones are professional and will probably ignore any information from the phone before they start fixing it.

However, are you sure that you want to trust the professionalism of a stranger? Also, do you really want the hassle of getting a new phone? Probably not, so invest in a good case and screen cover. There are many options for different manufacturers of cases. Be sure to shop around to come up with the ideal combination of protection and style right for you.

Putting It on Lockdown

Let's start with the basics of the Lock Screen. When you leave your phone alone for a while, or when you're doing something and you want to do something else, you can briefly press the power button to turn off the screen. This saves some power. Depending on what you want to do, you can make it easy or hard to return to using your phone by using the Lock Screen. The thinking is that you rarely lose your phone, or have it stolen when you're actively using it. It typically disappears when you leave it alone for a while.

To protect the information you keep on your phone, your S10 has the option of a Lock Screen on which, in most circumstances, you need to prove to the phone that you're you, and not some evildoer or a nosy family member. Figure 17-3 shows you a typical, and stylish, Lock Screen.

TIP

For reasons that sort of make sense, your phone uses some terminology that can be confusing. To clarify, the term *Screen Lock* is an option you can select to prevent unauthorized users from getting into your phone. The term *Lock Screen* is what you see in Figure 17-3 after enabling the Screen Lock option.

The most basic effort you can take to protect your phone is to put some kind of a screen lock on your phone. If you're connected to a corporate network, the company may have a policy that specifies what you must do to access your corporate network. Otherwise, you have seven choices, listed here in increasing degrees of security:

>> None (as in your phone will open up to whatever was there before the screen image went dark).

>> Unlock the Lock Screen with a simple swipe across the screen.

>> Unlock with a pattern that you swipe on the screen.

>> Unlock with a PIN.

>> Unlock with facial recognition.

>> Unlock with a password.

>> Unlock with your fingerprint.

FIGURE 17-3:
The Lock Screen.

You can select any of these options in the Lock Screen option in Settings. Here's what you do:

1. **Tap the Settings icon.**

   This should be old hat by now.

2. **Tap the Lock Screen link.**

   This brings up the options seen in Figure 17-4. You set some of the options mentioned in the preceding list and others when you follow the next instruction. This can be a little confusing, but bear with me while I explain your options and tell you where to go.

3. **Tap the Screen Lock Type link.**

   This brings up the options seen in Figure 17-5. Each option prompts you through what it needs before establishing your security selection.

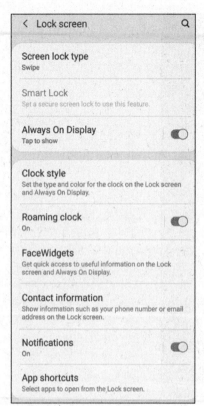

FIGURE 17-4:
The Lock Screen
options.

FIGURE 17-5:
The Screen
Lock options.

Preparing for your Screen Lock option

Regardless of what Screen Lock you choose, I recommend that you have ready the following choices at hand:

>> An unlock pattern

>> A PIN

>> A password

>> Your fingerprint

>> Your face

>> Your eyes

To clarify definitions, a *PIN* is a series of numbers. In this case, the PIN is four digits. A *password* is a series of numbers, upper- and lowercase letters, and sometimes special characters, and is typically longer than four characters. A PIN is pretty secure, but a password is usually more secure. Have them both ready, but decide which one you would prefer to use.

Selecting among the Screen Lock options

The first option of skipping the whole lock screen thing altogether is your choice. Good luck with that one *<sarcasm alert!>*.

The second option, unlocking your phone with a swipe, fools exactly no one and doesn't slow anyone down. Rather than just having the Home screen appear, your phone tells you to swipe your finger on the screen to get to the Home screen. This is about as secure as waving at intruders and tossing them your phone, wallet, and keys. The only reason to choose this over the first option is that you like to see, on occasion, the abstract image shown in Figure 17-3. Let's keep going.

I recommend drawing out a pattern as the minimum screen-lock option. This is quick and easy. Tap the Pattern option on the screen seen in Figure 17-6 to get started. The phone asks you to enter your pattern and then asks you to enter it again. It then asks you to enter a PIN in case you forget your pattern.

The unlock pattern is a design that you draw with your finger on a nine-dot screen, as shown in Figure 17-6.

The image on the right in Figure 17-6 happens to include all nine dots. You do not need to use all the dots. The minimum number of dots you must touch is four. The upper limit is nine because you can touch each dot only once. As long as you can remember your pattern, feel free to be creative.

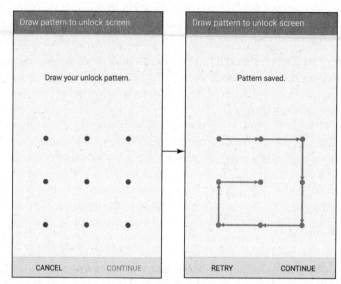

Draw pattern to unlock screen

Draw your unlock pattern.

CANCEL   CONTINUE

Draw pattern to unlock screen

Pattern saved.

RETRY   CONTINUE

FIGURE 17-6:
The unlock
patterns: the
blank screen and
a sample pattern.

TIP

Be sure to use a PIN you can remember a long time from now. You need this PIN only if you forget your pattern. That is a very rare situation for most people.

Each time you enter a Screen Lock option, two things may happen:

» If you've already entered a Screen Lock option, it may ask you to enter it. For example, if you've put in a pattern and you want to add a PIN, it may ask you to enter that pattern. This helps prevent someone from messing with your Screen Lock.

» After you enter your PIN, password, or whatever, your phone may ask if you want to save the pattern to your Samsung Account, as shown in Figure 17-7. It can't hurt, so you may as well do it.

Back up your Patterns?

Remote unlock will be turned on in Find My Mobile and your PIN, pattern, or password will be securely stored by Samsung. This allows you to unlock your phone in case you forget your unlock method. It also allows you to control a lost phone remotely, even when it's locked. You'll need to sign in to your Samsung account first.

To continue, read and agree to the Privacy Policy.

Agree

FIGURE 17-7:
The option to
back up your
patterns.

The next two options on the Screen Lock screen, PIN and Password, are more secure, but only as long as you avoid the obvious choices. If you insist upon using the PIN "0000" or "1111" or the word "password" as your password, don't waste your time. It's standard operating procedure within the typical den of thieves to try these sequences first. That's because so many people use these obvious choices.

WARNING

If, someday, you forget your pattern, your PIN, or your password, the only option is to do a complete reset of your phone back to original factory settings. In such a case, all your texts and stored files will be lost. Try to avoid this fate: Remember your pattern, PIN, or password.

Entering your face

Facial recognition is even easier! From the Lock Screen page, tap the toggle button by Face Recognition. You'll be prompted to hold the phone toward your face. The recognition screens are shown in Figure 17-8. They work remarkably fast.

FIGURE 17-8:
The facial recognition screen for Mona Lisa.

When your phone has your face in its memory, it will ask you if you want some options to make it work well, as shown in Figure 17-9. Pick the ones you want, and you're set. All you need to do is hold up your phone when prompted, and it'll know that it's you, and you're in!

Useful features

Stay on Lock screen
When you unlock with face recognition, stay on the Lock screen until you swipe.

Faster recognition
Faster recognition improves speed but reduces security, increasing the possibility of a video or image being incorrectly recognized as your face.

Lift to wake
Wake up your phone by picking it up. Face recognition will be ready as soon as you pick up your phone, without a swipe or key press.

Brighten screen
Increase screen brightness temporarily so your face can be recognized in the dark.

FIGURE 17-9:
Useful features for facial recognition.

Entering your fingerprints

Using your fingerprint to unlock your phone is very convenient and very effective. There are a few hoops you need to make this happen. You need to give your phone enough views of the finger you will use, which can be whichever finger you like, so that it is sure that it is you. It also wants to make sure that you, and only you, have stored a fingerprint. Your phone can store multiple fingers. Any of your fingers will work, so have at it.

Here's what you do:

1. **Tap the toggle option next to the Fingerprints option shown in Figure 17-5.**

   The leftmost screen in Figure 17-10 appears if you have an S10 or S10+. It's a little different if you have an S10E, where the Power button is the fingerprint reader.

2. **Press the fingerprint icon on the screen if you have an S10 or S10+. Run your finger over the Power button on the right side if you have an S10E.**

   Keep following the directions on the screen for how it wants you to move until you reach 100 percent. The screen in the middle of Figure 17-10 will eventually turn completely green, and then you're at 100 percent.

   Enjoy this keen sense of accomplishment, because in a moment, you will be returned to a screen like the one shown in Figure 17-4, but now has one stored fingerprint.

Your fingerprint is now in memory and ready to let you get to your home page with a quick press or swipe. Give it a try. It is very slick!

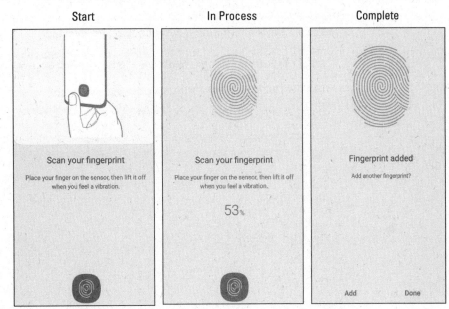

Start | In Process | Complete

FIGURE 17-10:
The Fingerprints registration screen.

Encrypting Your SD Card

This is an option to protect the data on your device. It's an exceptionally secure option: It scrambles every file on your microSD card into gibberish, which it rapidly descrambles when you need the information. This sounds great; in practice, however, there are some important considerations to think about.

First, all this scrambling and descrambling takes processing power away from other things, such as running the apps. The loss is hardly noticeable in most cases — your phone is awash in processing power — but you never know when it may come back to bite you.

WARNING

After you encrypt your SD card, you can never switch it back to non-encrypted. With the Screen Lock options, you can use a PIN for a while, and then switch back to the pattern if you want, and live dangerously with the swipe option until you go to a password. Not so with the encryption option. You will never, ever, ever, ever get it back together.

If you encrypt your SD card and then forget your password, your SD card is toast. You won't be able to use these files ever again. Likewise, if you ever need to reset your phone to factory default settings, it won't remember how to talk to this SD card. Once again, toast is the word to describe the SD card and the data on it.

If you're sure that encryption is for you, here are the steps:

1. **From the Settings screen, select the Biometrics and Security option.**

2. **Tap the Encrypt SD Card link.**

   Doing so brings up the warning screen, as shown in Figure 17-11.

   As the screen says, have your battery nicely charged, say, at 80 percent or higher, and an hour set aside when you don't need to use your phone.

<FIGURE 17-11:
The encryption
warning screen.

> ⟨ **ENCRYPT SD CARD**
>
> You can encrypt SD cards. Encrypted SD cards can only be read on the device used to encrypt them. Tap ENCRYPT SD CARD to start the encryption process.
>
> Encryption could take an hour or more. Before you start, make sure that the battery is charged and keep the device plugged in until encryption is complete. During the encryption process, the SD card cannot be used. If your device is reset to factory default settings, it will be unable to read encrypted SD cards.
>
> **ENCRYPT SD CARD**

3. **Tap the Encrypt SD Card option.**

   And off it goes. . . .

Keep in mind that this encryption is just for the data on your SD card. This does not touch the data that is stored on your phone.

Using Knox to Make Your Phone as Secure as Fort Knox

It doesn't matter whether you bought the phone at a retail store or your company supplied it to you. The fact of the matter is that company data that resides on your phone belongs to your employer. You probably signed a document (now sitting in your HR file) that states that you agree with this arrangement.

This policy is necessary for the company because it has a financial and legal obligation to protect company data, particularly if it pertains to individual customers. Like it or not, this obligation trumps your sense of privacy over the phone you bought and (still) pay for. If this really gets under your skin, you can always carry two smartphones: one for business and one for personal use. This solves the problem, but it's a hassle.

However, there is a better way. Samsung has a highly skilled group that has developed a secure system called *Knox.* Knox logically divides your phone into two modes: one for business use and the other for your personal use. You tap an icon, and you're in business mode. You tap another icon, and you're in personal mode. Switching between the two is instant, and Knox keeps the information from each mode separate.

TIP

This is a capability that is only of interest to you if your employer offers support for the service.

When it is available, Knox comes with three capabilities for the employer:

>> Security for the Android OS.

>> Limitations on the applications that access the business side of your phone.

>> Remote mobile-device management.

This arrangement means that your employer can remotely control the business apps and potentially wipe the data on the business side at its discretion — but it has nothing to do with your personal information. The personal side remains your responsibility.

TIP

You may want to suggest to your company's IT department that it look into supporting Knox. Doing so can take a burden off your back.

Being Careful with Bluetooth

In Chapter 3, I looked at syncing your phone with Bluetooth devices. I did not mention the potential for security risk at that point. I do it now.

Some people are concerned that people with a radio scanner can listen in on their voice calls. This was possible, but not easy, in the early days of mobile phone use. Your Galaxy S10 can use only digital systems, so picking your conversation out of the air is practically impossible.

Some people are concerned that a radio scanner and a computer can pick up your data connection. It's not that simple. Maybe the NSA could get some of your data that way using complicated supercomputing algorithms, but it's much easier for thieves and pranksters to use wired communications to access the accounts of the folks who use "0000" as their PIN and "password" or "password1" as their password.

Perhaps the greatest vulnerability your phone faces is called *bluejacking*, which involves using some simple tricks to gain access to your phone via Bluetooth.

Do a test: The next time you're in a public place, such as a coffee shop, a restaurant, or a train station, turn on Bluetooth. Tap the button that makes you visible to all Bluetooth devices and then tap Scan. While your Bluetooth device is visible, you'll see all the other Bluetooth devices in your vicinity. You'll probably find lots of them. If not, try this at an airport. Wow!

If you were trying to pair with another Bluetooth device, you'd be prompted to see whether you're willing to accept connection to that device. In this case, you are not.

However, a hacker will see that you are open for pairing and take this opportunity to use the PIN 0000 to make a connection. When you're actively pairing, your Bluetooth device won't accept an unknown device's offer to pair. But if your device is both unpaired and visible, hackers can fool your Bluetooth device and force a connection.

After a connection is established, all your information is available to the hackers to use as they will. Here are the steps to protect yourself:

>> **Don't pair your phone to another Bluetooth device in a public place.**
Believe it or not, crooks go to public places to look for phones in pairing mode. When they pair with a phone, they look for interesting data to steal. It would be nice if these people had more productive hobbies, like Parkour or searching for Bigfoot. However, as long as these folks are out there, it is safer to pair your Bluetooth device in a not-so-public place.

- » **Make sure that you know the name of the device with which you want to pair.** You should pair only with that device. Decline if you are not sure or if other Bluetooth devices offer to connect.

- » **Shorten the default time-out setting.** The default is that you will be visible for two minutes. However, you can go into the menu settings and change the option for Visible Time-out to whatever you want. Make this time shorter than two minutes. *Don't set it to Never Time Out.* This is like leaving the windows open and the keys in the ignition on your Cadillac Escalade. A shorter time of visibility means that you have to be vigilant for less time.

- » **From time to time, check the names of the devices that are paired to your device.** If you don't recognize the name of a device, click the Settings icon to the right of the unfamiliar name and unpair it. Some damage may have been done by the intruder, but with any luck, you've nipped it in the bud.

Here's an important point: When handled properly, Bluetooth is as secure as can be. However, a few mistakes can open you up to human vermin with more technical knowledge than decency. Don't make those mistakes, and you can safely enjoy this capability, knowing that all the data on your phone is safe.

Protecting Against Malware

One of the main reasons application developers write apps for Android is that Google doesn't have an onerous preapproval process for a new app to be placed in the Play Store. This is unlike the Apple App Store or Microsoft Windows Phone Store, where each derivation of an app must be validated.

Many developers prefer to avoid bureaucracy. At least in theory, this attracts more developers to do more stuff for Android phones.

However, this approach does expose users like you and me to the potential for malware that can, inadvertently or intentionally, do things that are not advertised. Some of these "things" may be minor annoyances, or they could really mess up your phone (for openers).

Market forces, in the form of negative feedback, are present to kill apps that are badly written or are meant to steal your private data. However, this informal safe-guard works only after some poor soul has experienced problems — such as theft of personal information — and reported it.

Rather than simply avoiding new apps, you can download apps designed to protect the information on your phone. These are available from many of the firms that make antivirus software for your PC. Importantly, many of these antivirus applications are free. If you want a nicer interface and some enhanced features, you can pay a few dollars, but it isn't necessary.

Examples include NG Mobile Security and Antivirus, Lookout Security and Antivirus, Kaspersky Mobile Security, and Norton Security Antivirus. If you have inadvertently downloaded an app that includes malicious software, these apps will stop that app.

Downloading Apps Only from Reputable Sources

Another way to avoid malware is to download mobile software only from trustworthy websites. This book has focused exclusively on the Google Play Store. You can download Android apps for your phone from a number of other reputable sites, including Amazon Appstore and GetJar.

Keep in mind that these stores are always on the lookout to withdraw applications that include malicious software. Google uses an internally developed solution it calls Bouncer to check for malicious software and remove it from the Play Store. Other mobile software distribution companies have their own approaches to addressing this problem. The problem is that policing malicious software is a hit-or-miss proposition.

As a rule, you should hesitate to download an Android application unless you know where it has been. You are safest if you restrict your app shopping to reputable companies. Be very skeptical of any other source of an Android application.

Rescuing Your Phone When It Gets Lost

Other options allow you to be more proactive than waiting for a Good Samaritan to reach out to your home phone or email if you lose your phone.

There are apps that help you find your phone. Here are a few several "lost it" scenarios and some possible solutions for your quandary:

>> **You know that you lost your phone somewhere in your house. You would try calling your own number, but you had your phone set to Vibrate Only mode.**

Solution: Remote Ring. By sending a text to your phone with the "right" code that you preprogrammed when you set up this service, your phone will ring on its loudest setting, even if you have the ringer set to Vibrate Only.

If you know that your phone is in your house, the accuracy of GPS isn't savvy enough to tell you whether it's lost between the seat cushions of your couch or in the pocket of your raincoat. That's where the Remote Ring feature comes in handy.

>> **You lost your phone while traveling and have no idea whether you left it in a taxi or at airport security.**

Solution: Map Current Location. This feature allows you to track, within the accuracy of the GPS signal, the location of your phone. You need access to the website of the company with which you arranged to provide this service, and it will show you (on a map) the rough location of your phone.

Here is where having an account with Samsung comes in handy. Hopefully, you signed up for a Samsung Account when you first got your phone. If you did, you're signed up for the Find My Mobile at `http://findmymobile.samsung.com`. Figure 17-12 shows the Find My Mobile PC screen.

FIGURE 17-12:
The Samsung
Find My Mobile
PC screen.

You can see from this screen that my phone is at 935 Pennsylvania Ave. NW, Washington, DC, which happens to be the headquarters for the FBI. All you need to do is get to a PC and sign in to your Samsung account (unless your phone is at the FBI). You can tell your phone to ring by clicking on Ring my device. You can have the PC bring up a map by clicking Locate My Device.

I suggest trying these out before you lose your phone the first time.

Wiping Your Device Clean

As a last-ditch option, you can use Find My Mobile (see preceding section) to remotely disable your device or wipe it clean. Here are some of the possible scenarios:

>> **You were robbed, and a thief has your phone.**

   Solution: Remote Lock. After your phone has been taken, this app allows you to create a four-digit PIN that, when sent to your phone from another mobile phone or a web page, locks down your phone. This capability is above and beyond the protection you get from your Screen Lock and prevents further access to applications, phone, and data.

WARNING

   If you know that your phone was stolen — that is, not just lost — do *not* try to track down the thief yourself. Get the police involved and let them know that you have this service on your phone — and that you know where your phone is.

>> **You're a very important executive or international spy. You stored important plans on your phone, and you have reason to believe that the "other side" has stolen your phone to acquire your secrets.**

   Solution: Remote Erase. Also known as Remote Wipe, this option resets the phone to its factory settings, wiping out all the information and settings on your phone.

TIP

   You can't add Remote Erase *after* you've lost your phone. You must sign up for your Samsung service beforehand. It's not possible to remotely enable this capability to your phone. You need to have your phone in hand when you download and install either a lock app or a wipe app.

Chapter **18**

Ten Features to Look for Down the Road

With the power of your Samsung Galaxy S10 and the flexibility offered in Android applications development, it can be difficult to imagine that even more capabilities could be in the works. In spite of this, the following are ten features that would improve the usability and value of your Galaxy S10 phone.

Always-on Personal "Dash-cam"

Here is a mind blowing concept: Your smartphone can continuously record your location, the sound, and video, up to and including a 360° perspective at HD level quality. There are two obstacles to this application: privacy and cost. As mentioned in Chapter 14, the biggest issue with privacy/security is the human factor, not the technology. Cost is an issue. Today you can store a full day's video for about $10.

However, the price of storage is declining by half every year (OK, every 14 months, but I want to keep the math simple). In less than a decade, assuming that these trends continue, you could store every word, every bad driver you encounter (I am thinking about you, Mr. Paul and Mr. Madamba), every move you make, every breath you take, in a year for about $10.

So why would you want to? Well, for one, video is wonderful if you are a victim of a crime. Second, it is very handy if you are ever accused of a crime to have solid evidence that you were not there. Next, this information would be very handy for lost children or mentally challenged adults for their protection.

With scenarios such as this, it is hard to imagine all the possibilities, but the technology is here today and the costs are coming down fast, so it is not unreasonable to imagine that, in the 2020's, someone's Samsung Galaxy S10 will be used for this purpose.

Home IoT Services to Differentiate Real Estate

Much of the discussion about home IoT services involves individuals buying new appliances, thermostats, lighting, security, and other items. That works for home-owners. It can also work for apartment dwellers and new home buyers where the landlord or builder provides these services as a way to differentiate their offerings. Typically, they will offer a mobile app to access all this stuff. This makes it easier for you to adopt this capability without having to maintain it yourself.

New Delivery Concepts

Most of us over the age of five years old know our address. It is on our driver's license. It is where we get things delivered from Amazon.com and other e-tailers. It is customary to have stuff shipped to a real address. However, if you are homeless, a road-warrior for business, or simply social, you are not always at that physical address.

Here is the future: Your smartphone will increasingly be used as the place to arrange for delivery. You can arrange to have physical stuff delivered to where you are, rather than an address. Shippers know where you will be based upon your smartphone, and can deliver to you personally.

This delivery can be by a drone, but more likely, it will still be by truck. They can find you and get the physical what-ever-it-is-that-you-want in your hands quicker than you can say Jack Robinson (i.e., impressively fast).

Smarter Customer Care for Your Phone

You may not realize this, but your cellular carrier lives on pins and needles during the first few weeks after you get your new phone. This is the period when you can return your phone, no questions asked. Once you go past that date, you cannot cancel your contract without a lot of hassle on your part.

This is why, if you bring your phone back to the store reporting a problem, your carrier will tend to swap out your old phone for a brand new one.

Usually, you'll just take the new phone and walk out with a big smile on your face. This outcome is good customer care for most products — but not necessarily good customer care for smartphones. The reason? One of the most common sources of trouble has nothing to do with the phone at all. For example, you may have left your Wi-Fi and Bluetooth on all the time, causing your battery to drain too fast. You may have left your phone on your dashboard and cooked the battery. Or, through no fault of your own, you may have downloaded two badly written apps that conflict with each other, causing the CPU in the phone to run nonstop as these two apps battle it out for resources. The problem here is that unless someone spends the time to help you with the underlying problem, you'll be back in the store with the same problem.

At that point, however, you cannot return your phone. If you're sympathetic, or very annoying, your carrier may give you a refurbished phone. You walk out of the store, but without the biggest smile on your face. Unfortunately, nobody dealt with the underlying trouble, so you'll be back, once again, with the same problem.

No surprise if you start to think that the problem is with that darn phone. In fact, the store needs to listen to you about how you're using the phone and then help you get the most out of it. This is hard to do in a retail environment where the sales force is under pressure to sell lines of service and gets no concrete reward for helping you with your problem.

This is where smarter customer care comes in. With the proper tools, you can work with a product expert to troubleshoot your phone. Some companies specialize in understanding the underlying problems and coming up with solutions for consumers. This kind of customer care costs the carriers a little more, but it makes for fewer unnecessary returns of perfectly good phones — and for much happier customers.

Smartphone as Entertainment Hub

Today's savvy technology customer has at some or all of the following:

>> Intelligent Big Screen TV or Dumb TV with a set-top box for home entertainment.

>> Home Stereo System for immersive music.

>> Home PC/Laptop for home management and entertainment.

>> Work or School PC/Laptop This helps you keep home and work separate.

>> Tablet for the folks that find the larger screen to complement their smartphone.

>> Gaming Console for games.

It would be hard to argue that having all these devices in one would not have advantages except for the following realities:

>> Docking your smartphone to your big-screen TV and/or stereo system is not very convenient.

>> Docking your smartphone so that you can use a full size computer screen, keyboard, and mouse is also not very convenient.

>> The tablet screen size can be easier to view.

>> The digital music on my smartphone is great, but there are many people who still want access to their DVD, CD and/or vinyl collections.

>> Gaming Console still have better games than what are available on a smartphone.

There will come a day when docking becomes so convenient that all your computing and entertainment will come through your smartphone, and you'll connect to an ergonomic keyboard, a bigger screen, and/or more powerful music amplifier at your convenience. The elements are there today, but it is just not convenient enough.

Driving in Your Car

After years of tempting us in science fiction movies, driverless cars are now start-ing to appear on the roads. Several insurance companies offer you an app to store your auto insurance information. Some car manufacturers allow you to check the location of your car and lock/unlock your car. These are all a good start.

What about the car unlocking and adjusting the seats and mirrors when you get close without one of those bulky key fobs? What about communication between your car and phone that would more intelligently let you use certain phone features if you are in the passenger seat rather than the driver seat or, if you are in the driver seat, to give you the freedom to check some texts while the traffic is stopped.

It is generally preferable for car to have its Intelligence built in and run off the car battery. That said, your smartphone knows more about you and your preferences. The best of both worlds is when you're car your phone can collaborate to provide the best and safest experience.

Serving You Better

The smartphone is the mechanism that companies use to find a better way to serve you. This will show up in a few ways.

The first is in much better mobile advertising. There has been talk for a long time that advertisers can tell where you are and then give you ads or coupons based upon your proximity. This is just now starting to become a reality. It's still kinda clumsy. If you have been Googling, say, televisions, you may see ads relating to sales about televisions. In the future, however, your phone may tell you about a sale going on for Samsung televisions when you walk by the Sears store in the mall. That is cool.

Even cooler is to be told that that particular model is on sale at the Wal-Mart store and that this particular sale is the best in town by over $20. This can happen if you are doing research at the moment. It may be possible for your app to flag you if you have ever done this kind of research on the Internet.

The second way smartphones are enhancing service is by automating the order-taking process. For example, wherever you see a video kiosk, that company can allow you to interact with the information on the kiosk with your Samsung Galaxy S10. Some fast-food restaurants have installed kiosks so that customers can bypass the line to order from the menu. The items are totaled and paid for by credit card. The customer steps aside and waits for his or her number to be called.

This exact transaction could take place on your smartphone. You don't have to wait while the guy in front of you struggles to decide between a double cheeseburger or two single cheeseburgers . . . and hold the pickles. Instead, you can place your order on your smartphone and wait with eager anticipation to find out what toys are in your kid's meal.

Placing You Indoors

The Global Positioning System (GPS) is great. It can tell you precisely your location on the road and off the road. Chapter 11 covers how it can help you get to where you want to be.

There is a confession to be made. GPS doesn't work so well within buildings. Once you are in a building, your phone only kind of knows where you are. The satellite responsible for sending out signals so that your phone can figure out your position is no longer visible, and the GPS in your phone waits patiently until it sees another satellite. Until then, it stops trying to figure out where you are.

This is rarely a problem if you are, say, at your home. It is probably only a few thousand square feet. Things are altogether different if you are wandering around the Palazzo Casino in Las Vegas. At 6.95 million square feet, this building has the most floor area of any building in the United States.

You could be anywhere in the 160 acres of luxury resort space. It is unfortunate if the Carnevino Steakhouse sends you a mobile coupon offering a two-for-one meal to your Galaxy S10 while you are already sitting in the Delmonico Steakhouse. It can be a tragedy if you start choking on too big a bite of your porterhouse steak and emergency services cannot find you.

There are some efforts out there to come up with a better way to locate you when you are indoors. One approach has been to estimate your location based upon signal strength of known Wi-Fi access points. Companies that hire a large number of smarticles (smart people) are trying a variety of technologies to address this problem. May the best company win so that we may all get better location-based services!

Better 911 Services

The 911 system has been keeping the United States safe for more than 45 years. The dirty secret of this service is that the underlying technology used to communicate information on the caller's location hasn't been updated in a long time.

To put this in perspective, your smartphone is designed to work with data at up to 300 million bits per second. When you call 911, the phone that answers your call is designed to work with data at up to 120 bits per second. (Seriously. I am not making this up.)

Many states and regions are trying to address this problem. This effort is called next-generation 911, or NG911. NG911 promises to make the information you already have on your phone available to the people who are sending you help. This new technology is slowly being implemented region by region in different states and counties.

For example, most 911 dispatchers can't access the data from the health sensors described in the previous section. With NG911, you can set up your phone so that first responders receive your vital signs and EKG the moment they get the call to respond to your emergency.

With a larger data pipeline between your smartphone and the first responders, you can send anything that's relevant, including medical history, your emergency contacts, insurance data, and whether you have any protection orders against stalkers. All this information can help you — and it's available right away because regardless of where you happen to be, your phone is typically there with you.

Less Worry about Charging

Samsung is highly focused on addressing the complaint many consumers have about the need to pay attention to charging. The battery technology in the S10E, S10, and S10+ is denser and larger and the USB-C connector is much more convenience. If wireless charging is your thing, the fast charging with wireless is impressive. While there are lots of portable chargers on the market, Samsung went so far as to introduce its own portable chargers.

As it is, even with all these heroic efforts and multiple options, keeping your phone charged requires attention. The future holds the promise that one day wireless options will be so ubiquitous that we as users won't have to worry about this. Our phones will be charged and maintain that charge without the need for much attention or action.

Even as we as consumers get use to charging without having to plug in a wire, there are companies that want to make wireless charging even more convenient. There is a startup that is in the process of commercializing a charging system using ultrasound waves, the same kind of harmless waves that we used to check on expecting mothers and their babies, to charge your battery from across the room. What will they think of next?

Index

choosing headsets, 182
connecting to stereos, 186–187
considerations for, 181–207
file formats for, 194
Internet radio, 199–201
licensing multimedia files, 187–188
SD card, 189–190
Songs category (Play Music app), 196
sounds, recording, 194
speakers
about, 182
car, 253–255
Sports category, 123, 124
sports games, 161
Sprint, 94
starting
browsers, 108–109
Camcorder mode, 152–153
Stations category (Play Music app), 195
stereo Bluetooth headsets, 184–185
stereos, connecting to, 186–187
storing contacts, 93–95
Strategy category, 124
strategy games, 161
Street View option, 174
stretch, pinch and, 32–33
stretching, 110
Super AMOLED (Active-Matrix Organic Light-Emitting Diode) screen, 26, 140
Super Slow-mo option (Mode icon), 148
syncing
Bluetooth headsets, 57–59
calendars, 211–213

T

taking
pictures, 138–146
video, 153–154
tap, 29–30, 33
Taxi or Ride Service option, 176
TeacherTube, 203

Technical Stuff icon, 3
TeleNav, 169
telephone calls
about, 47
answering, 52–53
call log, 54–55
emergency, 56–57
headset alternatives, 59
making, 47–51
syncing Bluetooth headsets, 57–59
Terrain view, 171–172
text messages
about, 61
conversations via, 65–67
dictating with Bixby, 230–231
receiving, 69
sending, 61–65
sending attachments with, 67–69
Themes category, 123
thermal runaway, 23–24
3G, 94
thumbnail, 29
Timer icon, 142
Timer option (Settings icon), 152
Tip icon, 3
Tools category, 123
Top Charts subcategory, 121, 123
touchscreen
about, 29
cleaning, 29
double tap, 33
drag, 31–32
flick, 32
navigating screens, 31
pinch and stretch, 32–33
press and hold, 30–31
tap, 29–30
track, licensing by the, 187
Tracking AutoFocus option (Settings icon), 151
Travel category, 123, 125
Trivia category, 125
trivia games, 161

About the Author

Bill Hughes is an experienced marketing strategy executive with over two decades of experience in sales, strategic marketing, and business development roles at several leading corporations, including Xerox, Microsoft, IBM, General Electric, Motorola, and US West Cellular.

Bill has worked with Microsoft to enhance its marketing to mobile applications developers. He also has led initiatives to develop new products and solutions with several high-tech organizations, including Sprint, Motorola, SBC, and Tyco Electronics as a Principal Consultant with Phlogiton, Inc.

Bill was a professor of marketing at the Kellogg School of Management at Northwestern University, where he taught Business Marketing to graduate MBA students.

Bill also has written articles on wireless technology for several wireless industry trade magazines. He also has contributed to articles in *USA Today* and *Forbes.* These articles were based upon his research reports written for In-Stat, where he was a principal analyst, covering the wireless industry, specializing in smartphones and business applications of wireless devices.

Bill graduated with honors with an MBA degree from the Kellogg School of Management at Northwestern University and earned a Bachelor of Science degree with distinction from the College of Engineering at Cornell University, where he was elected to the Tau Beta Pi Engineering Honorary.

Dedication

I would like to dedicate this book to Ruth Allen.

Author's Acknowledgments

I need to thank a number of people who helped make this book a reality. First, I would like thank my literary agent, Carole Jelen, of Waterside Publishing, for her support, encouragement, knowledge, and negotiation skills.

I would also like to thank the team at Wiley Publishing: Katie Mohr and Elizabeth Kuball. Your expertise helped me through the creative process. Thanks for your guidance.

I would also like to thank Kianna Noonan of Otterbox, Cassandra Weller of Asylum Public Relations, Noora Ahti of Native Union, Claire Rocawich of the Max Borges Agency, and Joseph Kawar of SlipGrips.

Thanks go out to numerous people at Samsung who helped make this book possible.

Finally, I would like to acknowledge Ellis, Lindsey, Arlen, Quinlan, and Indy for constantly making me proud.

Publisher's Acknowledgments

Associate Publisher: Katie Mohr
Project Editor: Elizabeth Kuball
Copy Editor: Elizabeth Kuball
Editorial Assistant: Matthew Lowe
Sr. Editorial Assistant: Cherie Case

Production Editor: Magesh Elangovan
Cover Image: Courtesy of William Hughes; Background: © oxygen/Getty Images

Take dummies with you everywhere you go!

Whether you are excited about e-books, want more from the web, must have your mobile apps, or are swept up in social media, dummies makes everything easier.

Find us online!

f ▸ ▶ g+ in ⓟ

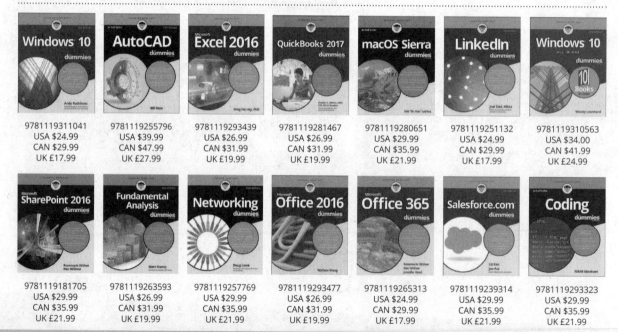